SHIFT HAPPENS

SHIFT HAPPENS

THREE-STEPS TO TURN CONFUSION INTO CLARITY AND LASTING CHANGE

THERESA COOGAN, PH.D.

Shift Happens: Three-steps to Turn Confusion into Clarity and Lasting Change
© Copyright 2024 Theresa Coogan, Ph.D.

All rights reserved. No part of this publication may be reproduced, distributed or transmitted in any form or by any means, including photocopying, recording, or other electronic or mechanical methods, without the prior written permission of the publisher, except in the case of brief quotations embodied in critical reviews and certain other noncommercial uses permitted by copyright law.

Although the author and publisher have made every effort to ensure that the information in this book was correct at press time, the author and publisher do not assume and hereby disclaim any liability to any party for any loss, damage, or disruption caused by errors or omissions, whether such errors or omissions result from negligence, accident, or any other cause.

Adherence to all applicable laws and regulations, including international, federal, state and local governing professional licensing, business practices, advertising, and all other aspects of doing business in the US, Canada or any other jurisdiction is the sole responsibility of the reader and consumer.

Neither the author nor the publisher assumes any responsibility or liability whatsoever on behalf of the consumer or reader of this material. Any perceived slight of any individual or organization is purely unintentional.

The resources in this book are provided for informational purposes only and should not be used to replace the specialized training and professional judgment of a health care or mental health care professional.

Neither the author nor the publisher can be held responsible for the use of the information provided within this book. Please always consult a trained professional before making any decision regarding treatment of yourself or others.

For more information, email theresa@tacticalchanges.com

ISBN:
979-8-89316-453-4 (Paperback)
979-8-89316-452-7 (eBook)

FREE AUDIO LESSONS!

This book is packed with examples, metaphors, analogies, and exercises to bring to life the concepts discussed in a practical easy-to-use way. This is a starting point to build and strengthen your toolbox of skills, knowledge, and practical techniques, navigating situations and contexts, and building meaningful connections with a variety of people.

If you're ready for more, check out the free 10-15 minute audio lesson series that you can get by visiting the Resources & More page at:

www.tacticalchanges.com

DEDICATION

This book is dedicated to two incredible people who continually inspire me: my dad, Robert, and my sister, Kathleen—foundational pillars of my support system and essential network.

Your unwavering encouragement through every twist and turn of my journey has been a constant source of strength, and I'm so grateful to share this experience with you both. Here's to embracing change and facing life head-on—Huzzah!

Dad, you've always been my guiding light. Your wisdom and values have given me the courage to chase my dreams with everything I've got and not be afraid to make mistakes. You taught me to believe in myself, even when the outcome was uncertain. I'm endlessly grateful for your love, guidance, and the foundation you've built for me and Kathleen. I love you, Dad.

Kathleen, my sister and forever friend, you may be younger, but you're a constant source of wisdom and balance. You've helped me find my footing time and time again, often before I even knew I needed it. Your humor—sprinkled with just the right amount of sarcasm—has a way of lifting my spirits and reminding me to keep things in perspective. And now, seeing you welcome little Mason into the world, I admire you even more. Watching him explore the world with such joy and curiosity is a beautiful reminder of what life is all about.

I love you both dearly. Your love and support have helped me uncover my purpose, sharpen my perspective, and ignite my passion. You've empowered me to embrace change, make bold decisions, and thrive every step of the way. Thank you for being my greatest cheerleaders.

SHIFT HAPPENS

Three-steps to Turn Confusion into Clarity and Lasting Change

Introduction xi
    Becoming Comfortable Being Uncomfortable xvi
    Understanding the Types of Crossroads xix
Step I: Finding Purpose 1
    An Educator and Greek Mythology 2
    Learning to Walk 8
    Gratitude Whilst Stuck in Quicksand, In a Dark Room, Without a Flashlight 13
    The Edison Moment 31
    Reflective Questions to Uncover and Find Your Purpose 37
        Finding Purpose at Work or in Your Professional Career 38
        Finding Purpose in Friendships and Nonromantic Relationships 39
        Finding Purpose with Partners and Romantic Relationships 40
        Examples of Purpose 45

Step II: Framing Perspective 46
    The 7 Essential Elements of Perspective 48
    Experiment #1: Making Lemonade from Lemons 61
    Experiment #2: Riding the (Tidal) Wave of Negativity to the Shore 65
    Experiment #3: Learning a New Language 74
    Experiment #4: Basic Math for Everyone 81
    Overcoming Imposter Syndrome 85
    Reflective Questions to Uncover and Frame Your Perspective 88

Step III: Fueling Passion 91
    Writing Your Next Chapter 93
    Advanced Math for Everyone 95
        Suggestions for How to Improve Sleep Quality 97
        Suggestions for How to Write Your Next Chapter 99
    Embracing the Change Process 109

Conclusion 113
Acknowledgments 119
Author Bio 123

INTRODUCTION

Hi! I'm glad to spend some time together talking about an experience that every person will encounter in their lives, myself included (and more times than I care to admit). What is this experience, you ask? Well, I'm glad you did! I'm talking about a crossroads in life. A point in time when you are going along, and then *Bam! Pow! Thwap!* life comes at you like a superhero from an old comic book with all the ironic comedy and tragedy it wants, and you find yourself needing to make an important decision. It's time to stop spinning your wheels and start making real progress. Don't just wait for change to happen. Make it happen. Embrace your power, take bold steps, and turn those moments of uncertainty into your greatest transformation.

Crossroads experiences can be positive and filled with possibilities and opportunities, like receiving multiple college acceptance letters, and now you need to choose where you will go. Or, your job has advertised a new position that would be a promotion for you. Your boss has encouraged you to apply, and you are interested. But, going for this new position might change the overall work-life balance and schedule to which you have become accustomed. These crossroads can be positive overall yet still include important decisions requiring us to weigh the costs, benefits, risks, and rewards. They require evaluation and analysis, and sometimes, we need more information. Even decisions with positive results can be stressful.

Unfortunately, people, when asked to share examples of crossroads they have experienced, more commonly recall examples that are less than favorable. These crossroads often stem from a crisis or trauma and can be challenging to navigate because of intensified and heightened emotions. These crossroads can seem gray or bleak. They can feel isolated and desolate. They can be disorienting and seem endless with a heavy veil of dread, despair, and sadness. I understand that even acknowledging this at the beginning of the book can be uncomfortable.

Together, we will discuss a three-step approach for navigating crossroads experiences you might encounter on your life's journey. This approach is designed for when you acknowledge that a situation, event, or experience has occurred in your life (positive or negative) and led you to a crossroads. You are stuck, feeling overwhelming chaos and uncertainty surround you, and a decision is needed to take action and initiate the change. Remaining in this state—when you feel like spinning your wheels, repeating the same conversations in your head or with your trusted friends and loved ones, or overthinking every possible angle—is no longer productive. You are ready to change but may not know where to start. Or, perhaps, you have tried to move yourself from this state of feeling stuck only to feel like you traversed right back to where you started from, or worse, a few steps *behind* the starting line.

It can be overwhelming and confusing to know where to start and how to start in a way that will reduce the chances of returning to that starting line. I can relate. Sometimes, it can be hard to tell if shift is happening to me, around me, for me, all of the above, or none of the above. I have felt this way repeatedly, navigating through positive and exciting situations and some very dark situations in my life. I have discovered that through it all, I can successfully move forward with purposeful and thoughtful value to my life when I follow three sequential steps.

First, we identify and then anchor to our purpose. Our purpose is the reason why. This sounds easy at first, but it does require intentional effort and courage to look within and truly see, accept, and respect the person we are for our beautifully imperfect selves. It demands a level of vulnerability and honesty to be successful. My training in clinical mental health and work in counseling taught me how to be comfortable in the uncomfortable. I will share knowledge, exercises, and tips I picked up in my career and life to help efficiently identify your purpose in a crossroads experience you are navigating.

Finding your purpose can be tricky because this unique element is woven into your authentic existence. It is your "fingerprint" capturing your beliefs, values, assumptions, prejudices, and truths. It is the key to unlocking *why* you believe what you believe and *why* you are passionate about what drives you.

It is that special ingredient that is true for you, and only *you* can identify what it is. Your purpose can grow, evolve, and refine as you live your life. What anchored you as your motivating "why" in your childhood will be different than what anchors you later in life.

By taking time to explore and identify your current purpose, which is now specific to the crossroads you are navigating, we can accurately zero in on our anchor point. This sets us up for success as we map our course for change and navigate the crossroads to the proverbial other side.

Second, we refine and frame our perspective while anchoring to our purpose. Knowing our "why" is critical to helping us understand, interpret, analyze, evaluate, and synthesize the information we already know and the information we are gathering.

Framing our perspective involves organizing our thoughts, feelings, and behaviors in ways that clear away the uncertainty and ambiguity, revealing a pathway (or, in many cases, several pathways) to consider for actionable change. Framing our perspective can result in a renewed sense of clarity and reassurance that this current state of feeling stuck is coming to an end. This becomes the catalyst and spark that lights the fire for the third and final step: fueling your passion.

Third, we prepare for action, leveraging our purpose and perspective to fuel our passion. Our purpose anchors our inner motivators and values. Our perspective frames at least one pathway forward that can navigate the crossroads experience.

I want to prepare you. As we begin the third and final step, we may not see across to the other side immediately. That's okay. By this point, we have the inner strength, hope, and courage required to take the leaps to facilitate growth and change. Passion ignites your inner energy, enthusiasm, and joy. It acts like a protective shield through a crossroads experience that often includes crisis, conflict, or trauma. It is reassurance and validation generated from within you, and I'll show you how to tap into that endless source of positive energy.

Life can be ruthlessly challenging one day and endlessly rewarding the next. Being a human is messy and filled with complex emotions, thoughts, and experiences. We are complicated creatures, even those of us who have found a way to master our inner sense of balance. This is part of the beauty of embracing the perfectly imperfect you. Recognizing and acknowledging you are at a crossroads, followed by finding your purpose and anchoring to it, framing your perspective, and fueling your passion, will help you successfully and efficiently navigate the positive and challenging crossroads life brings your way.

Now that I've told you a bit about what you can expect as you continue reading and we discuss these concepts further, I want to be upfront with you about how we can maximize our collaboration, because like the title indicates, *shift happens* to everyone. How we respond and make decisions to move forward when a pivot is required is what will separate us. I want to help you to be successful, and here is how we will do it.

I will tell it like it is. You are going to get the truth. No fluff. No sugarcoating it. My goal is not to try to sell you a ketchup popsicle while you are wearing the whitest of gloves. I won't try to convince you that the steaming pile of excrement metaphorically raining down during your crossroads experience is rose petals softly floating to the ground from a sun-soaked sky with white, puffy clouds and bluebirds singing songs. Oh, no, I won't be doing that.

I aim to help you learn ideas and apply skills through an easy-to-use three-step approach. My goal is to empower you to launch from a state of feeling stuck, uncertain, or overwhelmed chaos into a new adventure you are excited about. The truth can hurt sometimes, and it can also be the ticket to set you free.

So I say to you, I will lay down the truth in this book because I believe in you.

I believe in your abilities and capabilities to make choices that will steer your life in different directions.

I believe that if you get knocked down, you can choose to get back up. It doesn't need to be instantaneous or with a bouncy spring like Tigger from Winnie-the-Pooh. But I know you *will* get back up.

I believe you can make mistakes or missteps in life as we all can, and in the end, you will learn from them in a way that adds richness to your life.

You have the foundation to be courageous and add value to your life and to those around you.

When you put your mind to something and tap into a reservoir within you of grit, perseverance, and determination, you can accomplish the goals you set out to achieve.

Acting ethically, purposefully, and with positive intent for yourself and others will bring you rewards in life.

I am right here with you for every step along the way. You are not alone. You are never alone, even when it feels like the darkest of times. You have tremendous untapped strength inside you that, together, we will unleash.

So, we will stick to the unvarnished truth because, unlike Colonel Nathan R. Jessep decreed in a courtroom to Lt. Daniel Kaffee in the blockbuster movie *A Few Good Men*, I know you *can* handle the truth. So the truth it will be.

Becoming Comfortable Being Uncomfortable

My journey has not been linear, personally or professionally. The waters have only sometimes been calm and clear throughout. Can you relate to that?

It can be tempting to succumb to the feeling that we are the only ones struggling, having a hard time, or feeling uncertain. Even when navigating a positive crossroads, it can sometimes feel challenging to share with others, including those in your close network who you trust. I assure you that you are not alone. There is always someone else navigating a crossroads.

Here comes one of the first unvarnished truths—there will always be crossroads in our lives.

Crossroads experiences are opportunities for decision, action, change, and growth. By implementing the three steps mapped out in this book, the navigation process becomes more manageable. You become more efficient at adapting to a variety of crossroads experiences. Career-focused crossroads, no problem. Friendship crossroads, bring it on. Romantic-partner crossroads, let's do this. I'm ready. Personal development crossroads, I'm so in; when do we start?

We must be ready and willing to change to navigate a crossroads. The type of change needed will be different with every effort. Where you are in your life's journey and the experiences you have lived will shape how you approach and understand these changes.

Be patient with yourself as we embark on this journey. Remember, starting anything new is a change. You set the pace and call out the directions as we navigate through the crossroads experience. You know yourself the best, and we are untapping your inner source of strength.

Here comes your second unvarnished truth—the version you have been can no longer stay exactly the same.

It can be unsettling and even jarring to consider this specific recognition. The you that you have been, we'll call version 1.0, has served you well. Version 1.0 has lived through many experiences and has helped bring you to this moment.

The new version of you, we'll call version 2.0, is needed now and is moving forward. This is an opportunity full of possibilities. It is okay that it might be anxiety-provoking, stressful, or even terrifying. That is normal and shows you that you are still very much in touch with reality.

Think about a smart device or laptop computer. Even this technology reaches a crossroads-type experience with a barrier and an actionable change required to move forward. The operating system needs regular updates to address bugs, improve efficiencies, and enhance the device. If no action is taken, the challenges or issues will remain and eventually get worse. The outcome of navigating through the update steps, even with minor updates, is a new, improved, enhanced, and stronger version. Version 2.0.

Here comes your third unvarnished truth—even through the haze of uncertainty and the disorientation of choices to make, yes, you do know what to do.

It may not be clear to you yet. That is okay. Following the three-step approach, we will navigate together, and you will uncover the best solution(s) for you. Yes, that's right! Once you have cleared the haze of uncertainty and disorientation, there may be more than one solution to consider, so remain open to that possibility. You know yourself the best, and you know the best solution. I'm going to help you wade through the complexity to find it!

The complexity is sorting through the thoughts, feelings, and behaviors of that specific crossroads experience. Along the way, you are creating the new 2.0 updated version of yourself that you are becoming, with all the new features and enhancements like a software update in the latest cell phone. That extra sparkle that will shine in your version 2.0 can make others stop and say, "Wow! There's something about you!" I unequivocally believe if you have not had that experience, you will! And if you've had it before, get ready, because it's coming again!

As you work through the three steps, I have strategically placed mantras throughout the book to help us pause and check in with ourselves during the version 2.0 upgrade process. These mantras are a combination of sayings, quotes, thoughts, and feedback from others that have helped me. I want to share these with you and hope some (or most) will resonate with you too. I also encourage you to identify the unique mantras that come to mind as you read and consider each section. What are the sayings, quotes, and thoughts you have found helpful to illustrate those points?

> *Mantra: Every day brings you a reason to laugh and smile like a hidden treasure waiting to be found. Have you found your treasure today?*

Understanding the Types of Crossroads

I find symbols, metaphors, and visual images helpful when unpacking complex ideas. I have identified the universally recognized symbol capturing the idea of being stuck where decisions are needed to resolve conflicts, organize information, and identify action steps to move forward—a crossroads. An intersection of multiple points requires a decision that affects the course of action and direction for the future.

Regardless of the crossroads experience, the objective is an action that promotes growth and positive change and leans into healthy and adaptive aspects of living a rewarding and fulfilling life (even when a crossroads experience may feel anything but positive). Optimize as many days as possible, knowing that life is short and precious. You can make tiny changes today that will impact your life over time. I can say this with my whole heart and unwavering conviction because I have lived this! And I have seen it come to fruition in others I have worked with for over twenty years. This is possible for you!

We will navigate the three steps to uncover your deeper purpose, frame your perspective, and fuel your passion from a strength-based mindset. It may sound hard to do and darn near impossible if you feel like you are in a dark place at your crossroads. I have been there, too, and I have lived through it using a strength-based mindset. I will share tips with you on how I got to the other side and felt stronger than ever when I arrived.

Not all crossroads experiences require the same energy, emotional investment, or time. Each crossroads is unique to you specifically because it is *your* experience. Even if you and a friend are both experiencing a similar situation, like being laid off from work (as an unfortunate, more common example these days), how you each approach, navigate, and grow through that crossroads will be different because you are two different people. We'll talk more about how your essential network of people can be an important support along the way, and also ensure you are armed with your strength-based mindset to be successful.

Regardless of the crossroads experience you encounter, think of this opportunity as searching for a hidden treasure. The three-step approach becomes your map on your treasure hunt. I encourage you to approach this treasure hunt with childish enthusiasm, urgency, and gratitude.

Crossroads can also be moments we feel complacent, bored, checked out, or plateaued, as if we are robotically going through the motions. We might feel unmotivated, uninspired, or dull.

Perhaps you are in a job you dislike. Still, you are not sure if you should leave because you have a great work schedule, or you love the team you work with, or you can complete your responsibilities with your eyes closed because you've done the job so long there's no longer any challenge or new elements to learn. Or maybe lately it feels like the same record playing repeatedly when you have conversations with a friend or romantic partner. You think you've grown apart, but you want to avoid the conflict of ending a relationship and risk hurting their feelings. Perhaps you're thinking, *Yes! Yes to all those!* We can navigate through all of them.

Remember, this is not about other people's opinions or perceptions. This is about *you* and your lived experiences. You are the only one living your life, and the life you have is not everlasting. Living with purpose, perspective, and passion is essential to squeezing every bit of juice out of this fruitful life we have been gifted.

Regrets occupy space in our minds, hearts, and souls; they do not pay rent to take up that valuable space. Regrets do not belong. More often than not, regrets keep you focused on what has happened (or not happened) in the past instead of looking at where you are now or what is on the horizon and upcoming.

It is up to each of us to choose to understand, make sense of the information and context surrounding these experiences, and derive meaning. Every situation you encounter daily, and each unique moment, is an experience you can use as a springboard to derive meaning. Sometimes, these experiences invoke overwhelming thoughts and feelings that require tremendous strength, persistence, and support to find meaning and navigate to the other side. These experiences may feel more like inconveniences or annoyances that might discourage or disappoint us. Other times, the meaning may jump out at us in an unmistakable fashion, linking the experience's information and context and resulting in a deeper understanding of why and how we are in the place we are now.

No matter what the situation or context of a crossroads might be, it is a real moment when we have the opportunity to make choices and take action. Remember, not choosing—in order to allow things to remain the same—*is a choice!*

Are you ready to start our journey together, to unpack these three steps, and to navigate through your crossroads experience? As we identify and uncover your purpose (Step One), frame your perspective (Step Two), and fuel your passion (Step Three), I invite you to consider a specific crossroads you are navigating right now. Put these steps into immediate practice through your real-life example. I'll share examples from my personal experiences and examples from clients I've worked with along the way as well.

Here we go. . . . Let's take the first step together, beginning the exploration to identify our purpose as we navigate our crossroads.

STEP I

FINDING PURPOSE

Finding purpose is the first step in the three-step process when navigating almost any crossroads. Purpose can ground and anchor you when you feel trapped in a tornado of chaos and uncertainty.

I remember reading an article that described the center of a tornado as being very calm and seemingly quiet due to the extremely low pressure in that specific part of the tornado. This resonated with me because, often when we are at a crossroads, it can feel like a tornado of thoughts, feelings, and experiences swirling about us, creating and causing relatable chaos and stress. But if we can reach the center, there is a moment of calm clarity and you can gather your thoughts, harness your energy and strength, and use that temporary pause productively to reset for the next action steps: exiting the center of the tornado.

For us, we reach the center of the proverbial tornado when we find and anchor to our purpose. It might get a bit bumpy as we navigate the chaos to reach that milestone, but we will reach our destination on the other side of this crossroads together. Our unique inner strength and inner light fuel our purpose.

It might be tapping into your inner strength that will push a boulder up a steep mountain. It might be the intrinsic drive and determination within you that helps you take your first steps or climb out of a quicksand pit. It might be turning on the light within you, appearing as small as a tiny flashlight you can hold in the palm of your hand, with the power to light the world. No matter where your purpose resides, it will anchor you as you move with a clear focus in a positive direction. We will explore all of these possibilities and find your purpose!

An Educator and Greek Mythology

Humans are storytellers. Since our creation, we have communicated and connected with others and deepened our sense of meaning. Myths are one of the common forms of storytelling: people, places, and events that bring to life an idea, a value, or a belief that supposedly occurred at some point in the past. The underlying messages within each story often guide the listener toward a more profound understanding or meaning for connecting with others or living their life to its fullest.

A myth, while unsubstantiated as fact, can still be a powerful tool when navigating life's complexities. When I was in school and studied Greek mythology, I got lost in the stories, but I also appreciated how the characters seemed to be constantly evolving, adapting, changing, and growing based on lessons learned and decisions made. Sounds like a crossroads journey to me!

The person you are today is going to change and evolve; I can confidently say this to you, even if we have never met. Here's how I can prove it to you. First, consider who you are today, your responsibilities and priorities, what you hold most important in your life, and what drives and motivates you to get up each day. Now, shift your perspective to five years ago. How did you spend your time? What were your primary responsibilities, priorities, and motivators? The chances of these two profiles being the same are highly unlikely. I have seen notable differences within a few months during some of the major crossroads in my life.

You and I may not be precisely like the Greek gods and goddesses revealed in mythology, but we do grow and change due to our lived experiences and choices, like they did. If you're reading this book today and thinking that not much has changed in your life in the last year, pause and reflect. You've picked up this book because *something* has happened.

Maybe a curiosity to challenge your thoughts or to learn something new is growing. Perhaps it's hope for a concrete strategy to guide you in a new direction to shake things up and reignite a spark within you. No matter why you picked up this book, the point is that you have. Your interest is one concrete indication that you are ready now. Version 2.0 of you is starting to form!

You are ready to uncover your purpose and take action now. You are ready to consider and explore other possibilities and perspectives. You are ready to stop repeating the same thoughts, behaviors, or feelings and to replace them with new ones that will serve you better in the long run. You have ignited something within you that wasn't there one year ago, one month ago, or even one week ago.

Mantra: "Logic will get you from A to B. Imagination will take you everywhere." ~Albert Einstein

In 2013, veteran educator Rita Pierson gave a TED Talk called "Every Kid Needs a Champion." She shared a powerful example of when she gave a twenty-question quiz to her elementary class. One student's quiz answers were almost all incorrect. Ms. Pierson scored the quiz with a +2 and drew a smiley face at the top of the first page. After returning the quizzes to the students in class, this student approached her, confused about the grade received.

She shared how the student was confused because they thought they had done poorly on the quiz, and seeing marks indicating eighteen questions were incorrect supported that thought. However, the grade at the top of the quiz was written as a +2 with a smiley face drawn next to it. *This doesn't match*, thought the student.

In the TED Talk, Ms. Pierson described this class of students as a group who did not often perform well on tests, quizzes, or academic assessments. Even as young elementary students, they had come to believe the grade on a test was a concrete representation of their capabilities as a person; it was a part of them. A grade in school was a measure of their identity, symbolizing their abilities, aptitudes, and character for all to see.

This veteran educator disentangled the person from this point-in-time event, which was the quiz. We can have less-than-stellar experiences and rightfully fail an exam, but it does not need to define our values, beliefs, or abilities. A point-in-time experience or event does not anchor our purpose, and this can often be confusing amidst the uncertainty of a complex event like a crossroads experience.

Ms. Pierson, when asked directly by the student if they had failed, affirmed they had without hesitation, but she knew the test score did not define that student. This illustrates how the truth is not always easy to hear or what we want to hear, but it is what is best for us so we can find our purpose and anchor to it, preparing for meaningful change ahead.

She continued, sharing the student was still confused by her positive and outright cheerful demeanor while answering the student's questions. The unanswered question the student could not reconcile—*Why would a teacher be happy if I failed a test?* Her response—"You didn't miss 'em all" and "when we review this, won't you do better?" In summary, she illustrated how "minus-eighteen sucks all the life out of you; plus-two said I ain't all bad."

When we find ourselves at a crossroads, we often identify facts or information we believe relevant to the experience and assign value to those facts or information. This is a normal response in search of clear meaning and understanding during an experience void of both. The challenge is when we attach our sense of self. This can be a coin toss accelerating you toward your inner purpose or misdirecting you into a dark place of insecurity, shame, and vulnerability.

I have been offered employment at multiple companies and must select which one I want to accept within twenty-four hours, so I must have many valuable skills and knowledge, and they can see my potential already (accelerating toward inner purpose). Or, I didn't perform well on a quiz at school, so I must not be smart or intelligent (misdirecting away from inner purpose).

The facts of any crossroads experience are neutral. How we view and understand them and our role within the experience is where we begin to look for our purpose. Our sense of meaning, our sense of *why*, drives and motivates us regardless of the outcomes.

Life can be clear one day, and a big ole mess the next. Suppose we interpret and accept our experiences as perpetual examples of –18 all around us. In that case, we will feel we deserve the life of an endless obstacle course filled with barriers, boulders, steep mountains, and adversity, soon followed by doubt and despair. Instead, if we anchor to the +2 version of our crossroads situation, no matter what life throws at us, we will be successful. We will identify the purpose driving us forward, feel its solid and deep roots, and build our confidence and conviction in the coming steps.

Greek mythology's Sisyphus illustrates this idea clearly. The gods forced Sisyphus to roll a massive boulder up a hill, which rolled back down to the bottom as soon as he neared the top. He was forced to continue repeating this action for all eternity. If Sisyphus thought his worth and identity were limited to this task, and as such, thought his life was a lot of –18s, he would likely feel burdened by the repetition of what many might assume a thankless job and perhaps existence.

It can be easy to look at this context and say, "Now that is a –18 type of situation without a doubt!" Some may even let their own experiences and judgments influence and distort their understanding and interpretation of the situation, jumping to an opinion or conclusion: "Sisyphus must have deserved it." "If Sisyphus had minded his business and not revealed one of Zeus's secrets, he wouldn't have been caught and punished, which is the reason why he has this task of pushing a boulder up a hill only to watch it roll down day after day."

Finding our purpose means we seek to identify and uncover the +2 in the crossroads experience, regardless if we happen upon the crossroads experience by chance, accidentally, or as an outcome from a different decision or action we took. French philosopher, Albert Camus, author of *The Myth of Sisyphus*, used this story as his foundation advocating for people to embrace the present, find joy in the process regardless of the outcome, and accept that a never-ending search for meaning is a natural part of human existence.

Sisyphus found his +2 in happiness and peace from successfully accomplishing his daily tasks. He was not stuck in the past, reliving why or how he got to his point. He focused on the present moment and embraced it fully. The task he had may have seemed repetitive or boring to some, but for him, he reached fulfillment. He found meaning and purpose in the simplicity and productivity of his daily task: rolling a boulder up a hill.

As we seek to identify and uncover our purpose to help us navigate through a crossroads situation, we can start by asking ourselves and participating in the following questions and tasks as we disentangle the context that has led us to this crossroads experience:

- What is the situation, experience, or event that has occurred? Identify and name your crossroads. As you consider this crossroads, ask yourself if you were to take a twenty-question quiz, would you be a +2, a -18, or a different number? Or, are you at a hill with a boulder and a directive to roll it up the hill, only to watch it roll down as soon as you reach the top, and then to repeat your task endlessly?
- Keeping focused on this crossroads specifically, what are the details and views of the -18? What parts of you are activated as you acknowledge this information? For example, are you activating your values, sense of self, beliefs, sources of motivation, or other parts of your identity or character?
- Finally, stay connected to the activated parts you just identified. Now, shift your view to identify and uncover the +2 of this experience. As you engage in this task,

validate and acknowledge the inner happiness and daily accomplishment that comes with pushing the boulder. Validate and acknowledge that you have content knowledge that can be a base to build up while you strengthen your understanding and derive meaning.

You are starting to uncover your purpose! Hang onto that and let's go for a walk.

Learning to Walk

Every human experiences several milestones, starting as soon as we enter the world. During toddlerhood, for example, after learning to crawl and then taking steps to walk is a recognizable milestone. This milestone initiates mobility and movement as toddlers embark on new adventures.

Watching the process of a toddler learning to walk illustrates how meaningful change and growth anchored to purpose unfolds sequentially. First, the toddler needs to understand the experiences that have occurred (the past), then balance them with their current efforts and outcomes (the present), and finally consider their overall goal (the future). It also illustrates how, with each change, discarding what is no longer needed (information, energy, feelings, thoughts, or behaviors) to make way for new possibilities is an innate and essential part of the process.

This last element of letting go of what has been and may no longer be necessary or serve us well can be very challenging as we age. Like watching a child learn to walk, there are sequential steps to the process of growth and change. There is also a flexible timeline and varying degrees of complexity, ambiguity, or uncertainty.

Universally, patience and trust in the process, along with an undeniable determination to reach the set goal, are essential.

My nephew, Mason, is an excellent example of this idea. We watched him reach and progress through the developmental stages, where he learned to crawl, walk, and run. *How* he navigated these stages illustrated clearly the concept of finding and anchoring to one's purpose.

Mason was (and still is) an expressive kid. Based on his facial expressions and reactions, it was as if I was watching a silent Hollywood movie play out in front of me live. I recall when this adorable toddler (yes, adoring aunts can be biased) was having his own "conversation"—silent movie style—with my sister, Kathleen, as we were sitting in the living room catching up while Mason was sitting on the floor next to us.

Oh my gosh, Mom! You're telling me these things you keep calling legs sticking out in front of me when I'm sitting down, or that dangle down from the highchair when we're having dinner—can move?! And I can control them?! And make them move fast?! This is how I imagined Mason's inner monologue as he began to realize that sitting and rolling on the carpet (induced by gravity or not) were not his only options in life.

From the day he was born, and I held him in my arms while my rockstar sister took a well-earned break in the hospital room soon after his entry into this world, I could see his curiosity. His wonder. His innate desire to explore, question, and understand the process and mechanics behind practically everything. As he has gotten older, watching his preference to play with toys that involve creation, assembly, and destruction confirms his strong sense of curiosity in life. He is intrinsically driven to figure things out. It's part of who he is, even as a toddler.

When this toddler had his "ah-ha!" moment of amazement that he could be more mobile and do so independently, it was a game changer. Mason started by standing in place with support and assistance, walking with an adult holding his hands above his head and guiding each step he took. I remember doing this with my dad, but I would have each foot on top of his, so he was doing all the work. My, how times have changed.

Mason was taking tiny steps toward positive change and growth. When he began this journey, he knew his legs must be meant to do more than what they were currently being used for, but he didn't know precisely what that meant or even how to start. (We'll talk later about how trusting and leaning into your essential network of people can be helpful at all levels of the process, like how he leaned into his parents and other trusted adults to assist him learning how to walk.) For this example, the critical piece is Mason didn't need to make massive changes out of the gate. The tiny steps to start were having a big impact on the overall process.

He began anchoring to the reinforcements he was experiencing and observing. Yes, he can walk, and other humans are standing and walking, too. He had examples of those who seemed to have mastered this walking thing all around him to model. He had tapped into his sources of motivation to get a toy from across the room and to reach his mom's encouraging embrace as he shuffled from another spot.

When Mason decided to try walking alone, no one made a mad dash to fill out his application for the upcoming Boston Marathon race. Like almost every other baby, he started from a seated position, decided to try standing up, and began rolling and maneuvering his body into an awkward version of the Downward Dog yoga pose, struggling to maintain stability. Shortly after, gravity took over, and *plop!* Down he went.

He tried again.

He continued to try strategically approaching from different starting points—*perhaps the Downward Dog wasn't the best way to stand up; let's try rolling over differently.* Down he went.

He tried again.

Eventually, he progressed to maneuvering himself independently with assistance from some nearby solid object (or a nearby leg of a person) from a seated position to fully upright. He extended those hips standing up, supported by the couch, chair, or whatever he had used to counterbalance. Until he hit that moment, and like before, down he went.

He tried again.

He continued to practice standing up, refining the experience and reinforcing his intrinsic motivation and desire each time. He had found his purpose of courage, challenge, adventure, and adaptability through trial and error. He anchored to his purpose and *why*, his underlying drive to understand and explain why these actions had value in his life for his lived experiences.

The milestone was reached when he successfully took his first step, followed by a sequential set of steps, and in short order, he was running. When he runs, he often giggles, making sure everyone around him can hear how much fun is being had, even if he is running around the backyard because "the floor is lava." (For those who have not had the pleasure of imagining "the floor is lava," let me share that this specific inspiration Mason had stems from an obstacle course game show that showcases a pit of red goo that looks like lava. The competing teams must traverse a creative obstacle course without falling into the lava. According to Mason, at any time, a backyard can be instantaneously shifted into a similar environment, and the floor becomes "lava," leaving you no other choice than to use your imagination to run around the backyard, hopping on imaginary tables and rocks to "save" yourself.)

Now, was Mason gifted in some way, progressing faster than most toddlers through this stage of development, learning how to walk? No. He followed a very standard timeline many parents experience. I share this story with you because Mason's experience in learning to walk clearly illustrates how anchoring to purpose can ground your reason for engaging and acting.

Mason had a target goal set for himself (to walk). He experienced challenges and setbacks as he started and continued along his journey to learn how to walk independently (and eventually run). He fell a lot. Sometimes, it was a soft landing; other times, it hurt or startled him, and he would cry.

Did he think, *Goodness, I can empathize with Sisyphus, as learning how to walk is very similar to the repetitive process of pushing a boulder up a hill only to have it roll down to the bottom and I need to start back at the beginning, again . . . ?* No!

Did he think, *This must be my −18 moment, and I guess I'm just not cut out for this whole walking thing if I keep falling . . . ?* No!

Mason found enthusiasm, joy, wonder, and curiosity in the process of practicing repeated times. Mason demonstrated how commitment to a goal and task can enhance his purpose and value, thus increasing his inner happiness, not unlike our Greek friend, Sisyphus.

Mason viewed the entire situation as a series of endless +2s, until he reached the point where the +2 turned into a +4 and then a

+6, to achieve his goal. Mason was not distracted by a timeline or comparing himself to others. He remained focused on the process and chose the journey that was best for him.

By anchoring to his purpose, which was true to him, he not only accomplished the goal of affecting positive change and growth, but he also knew *why* he was doing it. He could experience positive success and potential setbacks with efficiency because they were tethered to his purpose. He knew falling did not indicate he could not, would not, or should not walk. Instead, it was an opportunity to take in and absorb the new information, balance it with what he already knew, and launch into another attempt.

> *Mantra: "I've missed more than 9,000 shots in my career. I've lost almost 300 games. 26 times I've been trusted to take the game-winning shot and miss. I've failed over and over and over again in my life. And that is why I succeed." ~Michael Jordan*

Gratitude Whilst Stuck in Quicksand, In a Dark Room, Without a Flashlight

Stay with me while we quickly detour into the wonderful world of science and physics to uncover concrete strategies for identifying your purpose. Navigating through most crossroads involves several twists and turns. Some of these unique paths guide you in directions that may, at first, not make sense.

Later in the journey, how or why they were a value-added part of the process becomes clear. Hindsight, in most experiences, reveals a clarity you cannot see when you are in the thick of things. Together, we will discover how to tap into that clarity while navigating through your crossroads and find your purpose for being on that path *and* your destination.

Let's start by talking about how quicksand, specifically being stuck in a pit of quicksand as a general analogy, can be a positive experience to illuminate how to uncover your purpose.

Quicksand pits may not be overtly recognizable and create an unexpected shock or surprise when discovered. Hollywood intensified this image by using quicksand pits to create urgent life-or-death situations for characters. In movies, these characters seem to disappear or quickly sink, as if being consumed by the quicksand, or to immobilize the character, keeping them stuck in one place for an indeterminate amount of time. Quicksand and quicksand pits are often generalized as symbols of sudden incapacitation and being literally stuck that heighten panic, anxiety, fear, and an overall sense of being trapped, usually in isolation. A few movies to credit for the dramatization are *Lawrence of Arabia*, *Blazing Saddles*, *The Princess Bride*, *Jumanji*, and *Indiana Jones and the Kingdom of the Crystal Skull*. Hooray for Hollywood!

With these illustrations and images in mind (and even more examples available within literary works that use quicksand as metaphors, analogies, and other colorful figurative meanings to capture entrapment or being stuck and often frustrated with an inability to escape something—or someone—persistent), unsurprisingly, many people will thereby interpret the idea of being stuck in quicksand as a negative and use it in that context when describing their situations or experiences.

I want to offer another way to think about this image as a symbol and a practical step-by-step guide for navigating through change (difficulty level notwithstanding) and how to anchor to your purpose. This understanding and shift in your thinking can lay the foundation for one of your most important and valuable experiences!

In many crossroads experiences, we will encounter our version of a quicksand pit. These pits are not all the same size, but they all hold the potential for similar effects. Learning how to approach stepping in, sinking, getting stuck, and escaping a quicksand pit can be vital to uncovering your purpose and propelling you forward in meaningful ways.

To reveal this approach, we need to take a quick detour into the world of science and physics and learn two key points. Let's start at the beginning. What is quicksand? Quicksand is typically found near river deltas, tidal flats, sandy lakes, and beaches. It is considered a colloid. The *Oxford English Dictionary* defines a *colloid* as "a homogeneous noncrystalline substance consisting of large molecules or ultramicroscopic particles of one substance dispersed through a second substance." Whew, that's a lot of science!

Here is the first key point we will leverage in our approach—an essential property of colloids is that the particles do not settle. This makes the sand feel movable, creating that immediate sinking feeling when a person or animal steps in it. However, the scientific properties tell us that even though that sensation is real, this colloid cannot form a stable solid mass. It cannot keep us stuck forever, whereas if we were stuck in a concrete pit, we would remain stuck as concrete forms a solid mass (don't get stuck in concrete!).

Good news! We are more than halfway through our science and physics detour.

Here is the second key point as we wrap up our science and physics detour. The more you struggle, thrash, panic, and let anxiety and fear drive your thoughts, feelings, and behaviors, the deeper you are likely to sink and get stuck. Many scientists agree that humans are likely to sink waist or chest level for an average adult. Conversely, if you can shift your thoughts, feelings, and behaviors to a state of calm and stillness (yes, literally stop moving), again, the laws of physics will help you. Your body's natural buoyancy will cause you to float, thus making it easier to escape from the quicksand pit.

Let that "sink" in for a minute (yes, terrible pun, but I couldn't resist). Considering this connection, can you identify a crossroads experience when you felt like you may have stepped into a quicksand pit? Did you at first try to resist being stuck and struggle or figuratively thrash and panic? When you reached a state of calmness, did you find it easier to see your pathway out from that pit?

I can recall experiences aware that I was at a crossroads, but I did not see a quicksand pit until I was knee-deep in it, and then *whoosh*, I was panicking and worried. How did I miss this in front of me? How did I not see this coming? Why can't I fix this or solve this quickly? I can think of crossroads related to careers, personal development, nonromantic relationships (friendships, acquaintances, etc.), and romantic relationships, when experiences like this have occurred at some point in my life. Sometimes, I felt a sudden, unexpected shift when things went from bad to worse so fast. Other times, the change was gradual until I realized I was in a lot deeper. Regardless of the speed of the trigger event, I unintentionally stepped into a quicksand pit and began sinking. I was stuck in an uncomfortable and limiting situation that tried (and occasionally did start) to insight panic, fear, and anxiety.

A common sign that helps me recognize when I am stuck in a quicksand pit is asking a rapid-fire series of "why" questions. You can tell how long you've been in the pit based on the number of questions you ask yourself or others, the speed at which they come, and how much space they seem to occupy in your head. Is this a main topic you think about and talk about? Caution, the longer a person remains stuck and continues to ruminate on the topic, instead of seeking purpose with a goal of meaningful growth and change like we will do, the more likely these questions will become unkind and irrational.

> Mantra: You are the only one who can hear the thoughts in your head, the good ones and the not so good ones.

The following are examples of many common questions that fill my head when I'm stuck in a quicksand pit. These questions can occupy space without paying rent and be loud, noisy tenants that create distractions. These questions become counterproductive; creating panic, reinforcing anxiety, fueling insecurities, and amplifying fear; keeping me stuck in the quicksand pit because I'm thrashing and struggling. I know firsthand how these thoughts can weigh heavily on a person, adding challenge and exhaustion to the overall process. Can you relate to any of these?

- Why did this happen to me? I was doing my job well, with positive performance evaluations, and others were not completing work on time or with accuracy. Or, I thought we were happy, and I have no idea why it doesn't seem that way anymore.
- Why is it taking so long to move on? I am doing all the tasks necessary for change. Why does it seem like nothing is changing for me?
- Why is it so much easier for others to make changes? What do they have that I don't?
- Why do I not deserve better? If things aren't changing for me and I am doing what is recommended to me to make changes and nothing is changing, I must not be deserving.
- Why can't anyone see I'm stuck in quicksand and help me?

- Am I invisible to others even though I've been asking for help? Does this mean they don't care or I'm not worthy of help?
- Why is life so unfair? How did I draw the short stick in life while others have so many more experiences, opportunities, and advantages than I do?

There is a glaring theme among these questions. Can you see it, too? We've already started talking about it. The questions that keep us stuck in a quicksand pit are all hyper-negative-focused and counterproductive to growth and meaningful change. Spoiler alert—we will also discuss how to combat negative thoughts in Step Two as we refine and frame our perspective anchored to our purpose.

These "why" questions and being stuck in quicksand—allowing movement, panic, anxiety, and fear to take over—activate and feed insecurity, self-doubt, shame, and blame. These thoughts, feelings, and behaviors act as blockers to deter progress, growth, and meaningful change. They keep you trapped in the same place—stuck in a quicksand pit.

The central theme is fear—fear in the unknown that I cannot control, doubting who I thought I was and what I thought I was capable of, and uncertainty about what others think of me and how that will affect my future. Fear is the common denominator of these "why" questions. These "why" questions are based on insecurities, but they are thought with such conviction they seem truthful and accurate.

Fear does not have an end goal of helping you progress out of the quicksand pit. Its single-focused mission and purpose are to keep you trapped, boxed in, small, and limited. Fear wants to hold you back from releasing your potential in every way possible. It keeps you questioning whether you have enough information to make a meaningful decision and take action.

When these questions become your constant self-talk record, you can see the effects on your mood, social connections, and overall health and wellness. Your mood may be more irritable or depressed. You may begin withdrawing from friends and family members, opting for isolation rather than engaging with others, even on a phone call. You may tell yourself you don't want to bring anyone down, so you're better off staying alone for now. You might feel contagious or like a walking bad-luck charm better off alone, saving everyone else from whatever germ you were unfortunate enough to catch. Your diet, hydration, and sleep habits are likely unpredictable and lack the quality to regenerate and recharge your body. Mental, emotional, and physical self-deprecating and self-sabotaging behaviors usually increase exponentially in this dark quicksand pit.

While I appreciate it may feel like it will never end, you are not meant to stay stuck in a quicksand pit. This is *not* your lifelong journey! We *can* make positive changes, and *you* can choose to begin a new journey.

> *Mantra: The grass is always greener.*

Here's how we combat that fear: Quiet and reduce those repeated questions, and effectively begin escaping from the quicksand pit. We lean into the opposite of fear—faith. This will take courage, vulnerability, and determination, and I know you can do this. Let's take the first step together.

Lean into having faith in yourself or a higher power (of whatever religion or spirit you believe). Also, have faith in the accuracy of the information you have already intentionally gathered to understand

and make sense of the current crossroads. Faith is the key to escape the quicksand pit. How do we take an existential concept and make it concrete to act upon? Here is where we can again take a nod from science. The objective is to be calm, relax, and stay still.

Fear thrives on chaos, reactivity, and continual (often panicked and thrashing) movements. In contrast, faith is nurtured by calm stillness, breathing, and relaxation. Let's be clear: Putting this into practice is often more challenging than it sounds. It will require repetition; daily is best but as often as possible is our goal. Remember that some situations may call for practicing multiple times a day. The good news is there are numerous effective approaches, allowing each person to quickly build a toolbox of their favorite techniques and to start implementing them today!

An excellent starting point for any person is implementing a simple and short breathing exercise called box breathing. This can be completed in as little as one minute, up to fifteen minutes, or more, daily. The versatility and flexibility to apply this breathing exercise is only limited by your creativity and willingness to apply it. I've learned that box breathing is also commonly used in some meditation practices and styles of yoga.

One of my best friends, Anne, who is more spiritual than religious, starts her mornings with a fifteen-minute meditation beginning with box breathing. She shared there are days when she will build in a five-to-fifteen-minute meditation or box breathing exercise during her lunch break at work, immediately at the end of her workday, after family dinner, or before bed. If she takes the train to work instead of driving, she might even engage in box breathing while on the train. For her it's a simple go-to technique that helps to quickly quiet the questions and repeated thoughts in her mind and to lean into her faith and calmness.

To box breathe, you are typically seated in a comfortable position. Anne described times when she had only standing room on the train, and it worked fine. Start by quieting your mind as best you can. Then, exhale as much air as possible to clear out the "old and stale" air effectively. This does not need to be like the Lion's Breath in yoga, when audible noise is made, but if that works best for you, then be your best lion! My exhales are silent and just like large, deep breaths. Now you're ready to breathe your box.

Pick a number between four and eight for your box breathing effort. If you are new to this breathing exercise, begin with a number between two and four the first time until you become comfortable with it. Work your way up as you become more comfortable. The number selected is your count, guiding when to inhale and exhale. The objective is slower-paced counting ("one-Mississippi, two-Mississippi, three-Mississippi, four-Mississippi," etc.). Keep that same number as you traverse each side of your box. Here's how it goes:

Box Side 1: Seal your lips and breathe in deeply through your nose, inhaling, letting your lungs expand fully as you count (by "Mississippis") to your identified number.

Box Side 2: Once you reach your number, hold your breath for the exact count.

Box Side 3: Open your lips, allowing the air to exhale fully for the exact count, letting all of the air escape in a full, deep exhale.

Box Side 4: Once you reach your number, hold your breath again for the exact count.

One box breath is considered one revolution of all four sides, including an inhale, hold, exhale, and hold. I like to repeat this process for a pre-identified number of rounds, usually three to five.

Anne's objective during her meditations is not to try and quickly convince herself that everything is okay. That is counterproductive and spurs the "why" questions to ramp up in her mind. Her goal of fifteen minutes a day is to reach or come close to a state of calm and peace from the questions, thoughts, feelings, and expectations she navigates the rest of the day. She knows that reaching that state of peace and calmness will automatically reduce the presence and frequency of the "why" questions as a natural byproduct of her leaning into faith.

When you do the math, applying a four-count box breathing exercise for four revolutions is only a commitment of 128 seconds of your life. That is all it takes to reduce or quiet the noise and chaos! Roughly two minutes and fourteen seconds is all you need to begin to effect change on the questions occupying space in your mind. Less than three minutes each day can start the shift from being stuck in quicksand to reaching the state of calmness needed to escape the pit!

Most people spend over three minutes scrolling on social media or waiting in a drive-through line for coffee or food. Where do you have three minutes to reallocate each day to begin changing your life toward positive growth and meaningful change?

Box breathing is a powerful tool that can transform your state of mind. It can help you shed the negative elements that weigh you down, like panic, anxiety, insecurity, and fear, and make room for the positive ones—faith, love, and joy. Even if it's just for a few moments, you can create a clearer, more peaceful space within yourself.

Clarity emerges in those precious moments of calm and stillness. In these moments, I've found the insights and connections that lead me to my purpose, like breadcrumbs on a clear path. Then, all I need to do is follow them.

Regardless if it is seconds or minutes each day, this is still time intentionally spent that will weaken the elements that create and maintain fear and instead empower those that foster faith. This is progress and change.

You may still feel stuck in the quicksand pit, and the change required to escape the quicksand pit may take longer than you hope or want. I appreciate that sense of urgency and have been there myself. Remind yourself change is happening! Your evidence of this is you are becoming calmer. You are relaxing. You are becoming still. This lets your body begin its restorative process and helps your buoyancy to float closer to the surface in the quicksand pit.

I hear some of you saying, "Okay, that makes sense for some crossroads, but how do I find my way out of the really dark and ugly crossroads? Because breathing doesn't seem like it's enough." I have been in those crossroads too! Experiences when I felt like I wasn't just stuck in a quicksand pit, but I was also trapped in a room with no windows and no light, and it was pitch black. In addition to the fear, panic, and anxiety that usually occurs when you're stuck in quicksand, now you get to intensify all of the thoughts, feelings, and emotions with a sense of isolation, disorientation, and a hyper-negative sense of never-ending dread for how and why you ended up in that room in the first place. Maybe you'll make it out of the quicksand pit, but there is always the uncertainty whether you'll ever make it out of that dark room.

A hallmark I've noticed in myself, to identify when I'm also in the dark room, is that in addition to the "why" questions (hallmarks of the quicksand pit), the dark room seems to bring a slew of "shoulds."

"I should have done this." "I should have said that." "I should have responded sooner." "I should have called." "I should have written that down." "I should have checked the work before it was sent." "I shouldn't have trusted that person to be dependable, honest, professional, and to not throw me under the bus."

Here is the best part about being simultaneously stuck in quicksand *and* trapped in a dark room—the exact science applies! Pause. Breathe. Check in with your body to relax, using box breathing or meditative practices that work for you. Find a moment of stillness. This is when change can happen! The change in the dark room, when you reach this moment of stillness and clarity, is when, suddenly, one small flashlight appears in your hand. It is a small change, but it can have a big impact on lighting the way forward.

Can this small flashlight brightly illuminate the entire room and showcase all of the exact steps you need to take? No, that is not a likely outcome. It, however, most certainly does begin to change your current situation by illuminating the first step.

You can see a new picture of the situation or experience. A renewed sense of control in an ambiguous or uncontrollable situation often emerges with this sliver of new light. The cloak of darkness and negativity is beginning to weaken. One small light to start the change process is all you need to build your confidence, to become calm and relaxed to float buoyantly to the surface, and to escape a quicksand pit (if you are stuck in one). This one small light reminds you that you can persevere and ultimately guide your pathway out of that room, learning from it as a challenging experience you overcame because you believed in yourself and maintained courage and determination.

> *Mantra: "As far as we can discern, the sole purpose of human existence is to kindle a light in the darkness of mere being." ~Carl Jung*

The flashlight may be physically small, but its impact and potential to effect change are priceless. The practical box breathing exercise can help when you are stuck in quicksand. Similarly, there is a practical exercise we can apply to help when we feel trapped in a dark room and want to find the small flashlight. We do this through practicing inward gratitude.

Inward gratitude helps you to calm, relax, and still yourself. It becomes the light. This light will always be more powerful than the darkness, and positivity is stronger than negativity.

It does not mean it is not without challenges. Inward gratitude while feeling trapped in a dark crossroads experience can be extremely difficult to implement and maintain. Prepare for this to be one of the most challenging obstacles you will face and overcome. Unfortunately, many will be allured to look for a quick and easy solution. Of course, this is tempting!

Here's another unvarnished truth for you as a question—Do we want hard now or hard later?

No matter what, to navigate through a crossroads experience, every person must overcome an obstacle (or many obstacles) that is hard. Finding your purpose (and later on, perspective and passion) *is* hard because you are constantly growing and evolving. What lights you up and drives you when you are younger is not the exact same thing at the core of the adult you. Introspective insight and being ready to reconcile what you learn about yourself is complex because it requires a unique type of risk-taking and vulnerability. Staying stuck in quicksand is tricky because you must slow down and adjust your speed, pace, way of thinking, and understanding of yourself and the world around you, intentionally and reflectively. Engaging in the process of turning inward and finding positivity and love from within, while simultaneously defending oneself from negativity, is hard.

Here is why we must take this step as we find our purpose. Inward gratitude reminds you that you are okay. Yes, you are in an uncomfortable spot, but this current state of affairs is temporary. Inward gratitude reminds you that you are stronger and more resilient than you think. It empowers you to persevere with courage, determination, and belief in yourself. Your "whys" of doubt, shame, and blame melt away, replaced by "whys" of curiosity, wonder, and enthusiasm for what is to come.

Exercises you can implement to practice and strengthen inward gratitude include thinking or saying something positive about yourself at least once daily. Once, my sister, Kathleen, sent me a care package for no specific reason. She creatively stuck Post-it notes on each item in the box with positive comments. For example, the Post-it note on a few individually wrapped face mask products read, "Let those rosy cheeks shine bright." She included two popular candy bars rubber-banded together. The one on the top blended coconut, chocolate, and almonds, and the Post-it note read, "Sometimes you gotta get a little nutty and have fun," whereas the related candy bar without almonds had a Post-it note that read, "... and sometimes you don't." Each time I looked at a Post-it note, long after the candy bars were consumed, those few words quickly conjured a smile and a sense of joy. Even the smallest reminders can have big impacts.

Think about the places where you spend the most time—in your home, your car, your desk at work, etc. Place your own Post-it notes strategically, with positive words or silly sayings and comments, as quick reminders at a glance. Then allow yourself a second, when you are going about your day and your eye catches one of those Post-its, to take it in and own what is written.

Another variation for those ready to go to another level is the mirror exercise. This is a timed exercise, and I recommend starting with no more than two minutes. In a location without distractions and interruptions, your goal is to silently look into the mirror and, literally and figuratively, open your eyes to what you see reflected. As you become comfortable, extend the time to acknowledge, appreciate, and respect the person reflected in the mirror. This exercise does not require speaking and often elicits a deeper emotional reaction than many expect.

An advanced variation of the mirror exercise involves verbally speaking positive comments and feelings and offering yourself feedback grounded in gratitude. Caution, while this exercise sounds simple, every client I've worked with who has tried it has shared they experienced an unexpected rush of emotions. Some cried, some laughed, but all ended their exercise with feelings of renewed peace, calmness, and regeneration. One client described their experience as if they felt they were a phoenix being reborn from the ashes! Be open to any degree of emotional effect during this advanced inward gratitude exercise.

Sometimes, inward gratitude takes much more energy and effort than we feel we have available. Sometimes, it doesn't feel comfortable to praise, appreciate, or show ourselves gratitude because we might not yet believe we deserve it. That is okay! Allow yourself to work through your quicksand pit and dark room in a place that's best for you. In these instances, I have an alternative approach that will still lead you to inward gratitude and strengthen the positivity from within.

We start instead with outward gratitude. When you intentionally engage in outward gratitude, you express how another person or group has positively affected you emotionally, mentally, and physically. Sometimes, focusing on others outwardly is a more comfortable starting point. This is not synonymous with gift-giving. Outward gratitude need not cost money nor take much of your time. Helping others. Bringing a smile, laugh, or joy. Being kind and respectful. Serving the community is an example of outward gratitude. Have meaningful conversations with people who have positively impacted your life, letting them know how they have affected you; simple gestures can convey outward gratitude.

Gestures can be as simple as holding a door for someone and facing them while doing so, instead of having your back to the person, or running ahead of a person to open the door for them when their hands are full. This intentional connection with another person, facing them, is an act of kindness that can be a tremendously powerful form of outward gratitude. Text messages sent without prompts to another person may include words, emojis, or a picture of sentimental value between the sender and sendee. Write an email or a physical snail-mail letter or send a greeting card. A live conversation in person, on a phone call, or a Zoom call can also work.

Helping others can express outward gratitude. Perhaps a friend or colleague at work has a major presentation coming up. Offering to help them prepare by listening to their dry run can be a way of being there for the person and expressing your outward gratitude. Maybe they're starting a new job, so you ask to hear how their transition is going and how they are enjoying the start to this new chapter in their lives. One of the easiest go-to's I enjoy is cooking or baking and then giving away what I made to my neighbors and friends. The act of creating and cooking or baking helps me relax and reset while being productive in the kitchen; and bonus, I also get to surprise others who have been there for me, helped me, or made my life a little easier with a ready-made meal or sweet treat.

> Mantra: "I've learned that people will forget what you said, people will forget what you did, but people will never forget how you made them feel." ~Maya Angelou

One of the common knee-jerk comments I hear when I offer this suggestion to others (clients or friends) is "I don't know if I can do that. It has been too long since [the event], and it wouldn't make sense to say something about it now." Or, "Telling so-and-so about how I appreciated their help at work seems awkward, and I don't want to have an awkward conversation with a work colleague."

When it comes to mind, the timing may not align with when an experience, event, or situation occurred. I also understand that some connections and relationships may be surface level only; going to a deeper level to express feelings and have an emotional impact is not a normal part of the conversation and type of connection you have. This is when acts of service, or small yet intentional gestures, work well. Outward gratitude is not about the size or quantity of your gesture or help; instead, it is about giving and service from an authentic and genuine place to connect with another person. The person may be a stranger (i.e., holding a door open), or more often, it can be someone you know (e.g., a friend, colleague, supervisor, family member, partner).

I have yet to encounter a person who receives an effort of outward gratitude and dismisses, minimizes, or otherwise admonishes it and its connection. The reaction might be confusion and surprise at first, but that only lasts for a second, if at all. Sadly, societal norms do not appear to align with expressing outward gratitude as a normal way of connecting with others in different areas of the country. It's okay if there is a moment (or more) of awkwardness to start. I have found that it usually fades away quickly and is deeply appreciated by the receiver.

While we all have our flaws and no one is perfect, being your most authentic self is the best version of you! Sometimes a response from the receiver is not instantaneous, and sometimes a response does not come. That is okay. Your underlying reason for initiating this outward gratitude is *not* manipulative or expecting something in return. It is an act intentionally chosen to give or send outward positivity, appreciation, love, and gratitude to another person or group. With this approach of offering and giving outwardly, you are preparing yourself to be ready and accepting of receiving gratitude from others and, ultimately, to turn inward to express gratitude for yourself.

> *Mantra: "In my life, I've learned that true happiness comes from giving. Helping others along the way makes you evaluate who you are. I think that love is what we're all searching for. I haven't come across anyone who didn't become a better person through love." ~Maria Gibbs*

The ideal state is to engage in inward and outward gratitude simultaneously. When we reach this goal, we open ourselves to giving and receiving from others while maintaining the healthiest emotional balance from within. In this state, you reach the pinnacle of clarity and capability for the most resounding impact and longest-lasting meaningful change and growth possible.

I like to refer to this state as the Edison Moment. In my experience, when I have reached the point of readiness to climb out of the quicksand pit and leave the dark room, it feels like I've had a lightbulb moment of awareness and clarity. This experience illuminates my purpose, which I anchor to guide me the rest of the way.

The Edison Moment

A nod to history to start this discussion: I'd like to give credit to the several British inventors of the 1830s who are well documented as the original inventors of the arc lamp. The lightbulb is an example, like most inventions, that involved several contributions by many people over time, each offering unique improvements and enhancements. However, one person is often universally recognized and credited for an invention. This is the case with the incandescent lightbulb where Thomas Edison is often recognized and credited as the inventor.

Let's talk more about this "lightbulb moment" milestone you will experience when finding and anchoring to your purpose. A frustrating point, I'll call out now, is that the timing of these moments can be widely unpredictable. It is also uncertain if there will be several small moments ("night-light moments") or one more significant moment (i.e., a lightbulb moment). I have observed a correlation that the more you intentionally engage in ongoing (and often daily) efforts to calm and relax while practicing inward and/or outward gratitude and box breathing techniques, the more likely you will experience these moments.

Finding your purpose is like a scavenger hunt. You continue to find treasures as you dig deeper and deeper. These treasures are insights into who you are as a person, your character, the value of the life you were leading, and the life you have lived. These treasures are the blueprints of who you are. We do not all have privileged journeys or experiences. We do not all have smooth roads to walk on. We all have unique treasures that make us who we are as individuals and unforgettable people. It's not always comfortable to search for the treasures that make us who we are or to find them, but they always exist and show you your purpose.

Characteristics of the Edison Moment can vary between people. I have personally experienced different Edison Moments based on the type of crossroads I was navigating. Flexible thinking and openness to any possibility can serve you well when uncovering your purpose.

Key characteristics to look for that will indicate you are having an Edison Moment often include awareness that the "why" and/or "should" questions, previously and distractingly consuming your mind, have lessened in their frequency, volume, and the overall space they occupy. The questions evolve from being rooted in self-doubt, shame, and blame to establishing new roots in opportunity, possibility, and determining prioritization (e.g., Should I do this first, or should I do that first? Why can't I get that certificate? Why wouldn't I be the best candidate for that job?). Thoughts that occupy your mind may still be critical-thinking questions, but their focus is shaped by their roots in curiosity and forward thinking.

At this point, you are aware of changes in your behaviors and how those behaviors affect you on any typical day. Feeling a sense of physical relief in your body by relaxing and releasing tense muscles changes your posture. You notice your sleep improving and not feeling as fatigued as before. You have unlocked your treasure chest, revealing positivity, insights, and uniqueness that are authentic to you. This discovery invites a more precise understanding of the deeper meaning of why you are at the crossroads and a clearer understanding of what has led you here.

Remember, when you find your purpose, it's not about right and wrong. Finding your purpose is not about judgment. You can analyze and evaluate without judgment. How we understand and define our purpose will inevitably evolve as we navigate our unique life journey. Your purpose encapsulates your values, beliefs, assumptions, prejudices, and sense of self. It is your view of the world around you and how you define the reflection you see in a mirror. It is how you self-regulate your emotions and thoughts to reach a calm and relaxed peace regardless of the contextual situation around you.

Even when we make mistakes in life, those who anchor to purpose will understand mistakes as learning obstacles that offer a lesson to enrich or enhance our lives. Mistakes are not failures that reflect our character, value, or worth as people. Sometimes, we learn the lesson on the first attempt. Other times, we may encounter the situation, the conflict, or personality many times. If it feels like a repeated occurrence, you are not doing anything wrong, are not unlucky in this life, and are not being punished. Progress and change are happening for you! And, just like there is for all of us, there is more room for learning, growth, and practice.

> *Mantra: "I have not failed. I've just found 10,000 ways that won't work." ~Thomas A. Edison*

Your environment can often give clues to help you uncover your purpose. In many situations, the group of people you spend most of your time with can influence your purpose. Your immediate environment can intensify your feeling stuck in a quicksand pit or being trapped in a dark room. Conversely, it can also be a key element in helping you find your small flashlight, shining it a little brighter, for longer, and in the direction needed to lead you to your unique Edison Moment. This can be understood from a holistic perspective, or it can be connected to specific compartments of your life (at work, at home, with friends, etc.). Undoubtedly, there will be crossover and patterns.

For example, suppose the environment and people with who you spend most of your time are often filled with negative energy, arguing, complaining, yelling, sadness, and reactivity, either by you or by those you live or work with. In that case, it stands to reason you might find yourself being more drawn to those types of personalities and environments. The negative perspective has become your current state of normal and thus where you feel the most familiar, even if it may not be comfortable. Being stuck in a quicksand pit or trapped in a dark room becomes comfortable at the peak of this environmental influence because it is the constant in your life. It becomes more anxiety-provoking to change or engage in any actions grounded in intentional positivity, love, or joy. You may begin to believe the negative thoughts, feelings, or behaviors that surround you as accurate, when it is unlikely they are. Because it is what you have become comfortable with, you may stay in the quicksand or dark room longer than necessary.

Conversely, suppose the environment and people with who you spend the most time are often filled with positivity, calmness, balance, laughter, and love. In that case, you might be more drawn to people, personalities, and environments that invite innovation, finding the fun in any situation through planned effort or spontaneity, creation, and efficient productivity. Having self-awareness to understand how your environment and the people you spend the most time with can help uncover your purpose.

A key element of self-awareness is understanding your unique energy source and how you best recharge and reset that energy source. Where do you fall on the spectrum of introverted and extroverted? When considering these aspects of an individual's personality, we seek to define and understand how the individual prefers to recharge and reset their energy source as the distinguishing factor. Let's unpack these personality traits and clarify where you derive your energy.

Do you find it practical to recharge and reset your source of energy in environments with other people, even if you are not talking with them? Do you recharge and reset when you can engage with them? Is it when you connect with friends and/or strangers? If you said yes, then you're likely more of an extrovert.

Do you find it more effective to recharge and reset your source of energy in a quiet environment with few or no other people? This might be your home with your immediate family members only, or perhaps you live alone and have pets. You may also find it helpful to be outdoors, engaged in activities but having experiences with few or no other people. You're likely more of an introvert if you said yes to this.

Remember, this is a spectrum, and it evolves. Where and how you derive energy, reset, and recharge is unique to you. It can evolve at different levels in different contexts and phases of your journey in life.

I'm a classic example of someone who started their journey in life as an extroverted child, and now, I am loving my introverted adult self. I am regularly mislabeled as an extrovert because I can engage in meaningful connections with enthusiastic energy and enjoy experiencing life with others. This is authentically me, but it is not how I recharge and reset my energy source.

A common misconception is that the spectrum of introversion and extroversion is based on how comfortable a person feels verbally communicating with other people. This is incomplete. I know many introverted people (I am one of them now) who can connect and have conversations with a variety of people individually, in small groups, or in large banquet halls facilitating a keynote session at a national conference. I can be energetic, enthusiastic, animated, and engaging throughout the connection, genuinely and authentically present in that conversation and connective experience. And, most of the time, these situations wipe me out! I get back to my car, home, or hotel room if I'm traveling for a training or speaking event, and I just want to sleep or sit in silence. Scratch that—I *need* to sleep or sit in silence to recharge. My proverbial battery that was at 100 percent has been effectively drained, and sometimes the experience could only be an hour or two. My source of energy and how I maintain it is how I know I am more of an introvert.

To recharge my energy, I love being home with my family or by myself and a sassy rescue pit bull called Maze. I enjoy spending time outside, often alone, playing in the dirt of the garden I've tried to build in the backyard and attempting to grow vegetables and herbs (although I have not yet discovered a green thumb at all). I enjoy cooking and baking in the kitchen, sometimes with music, sometimes without, sometimes with spontaneous dance parties with or without the dog. I enjoy reading a book or sometimes watching a movie or show. I recharge quickly when I go on walks (or, more recently, runs; thank you, fitness family) around the neighborhood or on nearby greenways. Any time of day, any day of the week, these go-to's will be my proverbial energy charging cords, skyrocketing me up to 100 percent faster than my cell phone charger works. There are some instances when smaller groups of people or specific environments can be recharging, but overall, my primary sources are tried and steadfast anchors to my introverted self.

Examining how your sense of purpose, value, and worth are all influenced by how you derive your energy, the energy of those around you, and who you engage with can most often teach you a lot about yourself. We do not always get to choose these groups of people, as is the case with family for most. We can, however, choose how we engage, derive energy, and ultimately influence our purpose and meaning.

> *Mantra: "You're the average of the five people you spend the most time with." ~Jim Rohn*

Reflective Questions to Uncover and Find Your Purpose

It's time to clarify and anchor your purpose as we navigate your crossroads. Let's start by focusing on the crossroads you identified as most relevant for you and clarify it through the various analogies and symbolism we explored. Here are some reflective questions to consider:

- Do you feel like Sisyphus pushing a boulder up a hillside right now? If so, what is the boulder you're carrying? What hillside are you climbing? As you look around, how high up the mountain are you and what does the surrounding scenery look like?
- If you were to take a quiz on your current crossroads situation, would you grade yourself at a −18 or a +2?
- Where are you in your journey of learning how to walk? Have you just discovered your legs are body parts that can hold you upright when you stand? Have you taken your first step and fallen? Have you gotten back up yet, after having fallen?
- Do you feel like you are stuck in a pit of quicksand? If so, are you calm and relaxed or in the process of floating to the surface?
- Do you feel like you are trapped in a dark room? Can you still feel the small flashlight in your hand? Is it on? What do you see when you shine it?
- Have you experienced an Edison Moment specific to this crossroads? If so, what was it? How did you know it occurred?
- Where is your energy source most often rooted when recharging or resetting? Are you more on the introverted side of the spectrum or the extroverted side?

- What are the environments, people, or types of personalities you spend the most time with? Being completely honest with yourself, how does each affect your thoughts, feelings, and behaviors? Is this aligned with what you want moving forward?

Now, let's focus again on your crossroads, but this time, look inward. Trust yourself to know the answers to these questions. You already know the truth; you just need to say it, believe it, and own it.

With the common categories of crossroads I encounter personally and with clients, here are some guiding questions to help get you started and organized. You can mix and match questions as they feel relevant to your unique crossroads, and you may identify your own questions, too.

Be as specific and honest with yourself as you consider these questions. Be open to the new questions and insights popping up for you as you contemplate these questions. It may be helpful to plan to engage in this reflection after meditating or when you are free of distractions and can take the uninterrupted time you need to explore and consider. It may help to write down your responses, to return to them later, and to reflect more and invite your Edison Moment to shine. There is no magic time frame to complete this for successful or optimal results. Remember, it is about the journey and the process. No matter your purpose, trust in yourself to guide this unique experience and the crossroads you are now navigating.

Finding Purpose at Work or in Your Professional Career

- What are the top three recurring emotions you feel as you navigate this crossroads? Once you have identified them,

rank them from the most profound and resounding impact to the least.
- What is the ideal work environment where you do your best work or have the most productivity?
- What will you never compromise on?
- What type of job or environment excites you into considering waking up each day to engage in?
- Have you ever felt like you engaged in work or a hobby that felt effortless, and time didn't exist because you were so wrapped up and consumed with positive joy in the work or hobby itself? If so, what was it?

Finding Purpose in Friendships and Nonromantic Relationships

- As you reflect on a specific friendship or nonromantic relationship, what are examples of when you felt most like yourself? What were you doing? What are the patterns among these examples?
- When did you feel most empowered to grow and take healthy risks to better yourself because you knew a friendship or a nonromantic relationship supported you?
- When did you find yourself at the peak of creativity, drive, and energy?
- Do you find yourself compelled to fix, solve, or guide others' decisions and lives as your role in the relationship? Or is there a balance where you grow along with the other person?

Finding Purpose with Partners and Romantic Relationships

- What are the most stable and dependable aspects of your relationship?
- What do you love most about yourself as a part of this relationship?
- What do you love most about relationships and partnerships?
- What do you need to grow?
- Is the frequency and volume of what you need for growth at a level that currently supports that outcome?
- How do you communicate with your partner when most challenged by your crossroads?

By answering any of these probing questions, you are uncovering your purpose. Your purpose is a way to capture your values, beliefs, and reasons unique to you. It anchors the choices and decisions to be made that are still ahead.

As you answer the questions, identify the themes and patterns.

Here is how I found my purpose when I experienced a career-related crossroads. I was employed at a large company and felt myself sinking deeper and deeper into the quicksand pit. For some time I didn't even realize it was happening. My jolted experience that helped me recognize I was stuck was noticing the patterns I had developed. It started by recognizing I always felt fatigued, and even my go-to recharging strategies, like cooking and baking, now felt like work and an obligation. It opened my awareness that my creativity, innovative curiosity, and general positive outlook had dimmed substantially. I began to notice my sleep habits were inconsistent and lacked any restorative quality.

The Sunday scaries seemed to happen on every day that ended in a y without fail. I loathed department and group meetings because the first half of every meeting would inevitably be spent in a group discussion complaining or talking specifically about "barriers" and "roadblocks" with no real effort to solve them. Instead, the leadership and group dynamics appeared to value and generate outcomes that reinforced the frustrating aspects, created or caused. The phrase "death by meetings" took on a new meaning for me in this experience.

Looking in the mirror, I saw a tired, unmotivated, and sometimes truly unrecognizable woman staring back at me. That was a very unsettling moment when I didn't recognize the person I saw in the mirror. I was surrounded by a suffocating amount of negativity weighing me down. My Edison Moment came in multiple ways, and as I began to embrace and practice calming, relaxing, and inward gratitude, the frequency and clarity of each Edison Moment were more pronounced than the one before it. In this experience, I needed multiple Edison Moments because I kept dismissing them as if they were just figments of my imagination.

I had a job with steady paycheck benefits, and it met me and my family's needs. I shouldn't be greedy, expecting more fulfillment in my role or contributions. I shouldn't want to use more of my skills, knowledge, and experience to develop my talents. I tried to convince myself I wasn't settling, forcing myself to be happy with what I had and quietly doing my job like the robot the company seemed to want. After all, I'd almost convinced myself no one is happy in their career and no one cares because finding work you enjoy and that energizes you is unrealistic. That was an urban fairy tale. Right?

From this perspective, I can understand why I dismissed the small Edison Moments when they started coming. I had gotten stuck in the quicksand and a dark room and scored myself a -50 on a twenty-item quiz.

I began uncovering my purpose by starting with minor concrete changes. First, I anchored to balance and identify concrete actions I could immediately employ to help me reach that objective, effectively testing out if that was my true purpose. It was a "purpose test drive."

I deleted my work email from my cell phone (I was not in a role where I was required to have email on my phone and be accessible 24/7). I began implementing other strategies, establishing healthier work-life balance and boundaries for when I'd start and end work. No more 11:00 p.m. email responses or weekends spent on reviews, analyses, presentations, or reports. My schedule met the requirements for my job without question, and I gave high-quality work and effort during the hours I was being paid. I set a predictable and transparent schedule for myself, my family, and my team at work. I updated my calendar settings on the work system to indicate work hours and nonwork hours. I blocked off time daily to complete specific recurring tasks, ensuring they would get done and I would not be scrambling. I knew clearly when I was in work mode and when I was not, and so did everyone else. This organizational and time-management strategy supported transparency, communication, and balance. I found myself more productive and continued producing high-quality work with reduced stress and fatigue.

For those who say, "That is great, but that's a big change for me, not a small one," I suggest starting small, with one day, and building from there. Pick a day you know will be the easiest to create and establish a realistic and reasonable schedule. Trial-run it for a week or two, then add on a second day, then a third, until you have your full-week routine established. Remember, you can set up different routines on different days! What is going to create balance in your life?

Bonus: These balancing actions I took began to quickly and positively affect my sleep habits, increasing my energy and internal motivation. Creative and innovative ideas began to spark. The "whys," "shoulds," and my feeling invisible and small started to melt away. I noticed a change in my outlook, overall emotional state, and behaviors as I began celebrating and acknowledging the positives, even in the small things. The initial start with balance opened my first purpose of creativity and innovation.

I started seeing opportunities I had no idea were there before; yet at that point, when I finally saw them, it seemed like they had almost been there all long, I just couldn't see them through the haze of uncertainty and negativity previously clouding my sight. My small-flashlight moment was happening as I continued to lean into faith, calmness, and inward gratitude. This also unlocked a second purpose: service. Helping and serving others in so many ways fueled my creativity and innovation. And the more I created, the more I was excited to serve and give back, fueling my outward gratitude. Creativity and service were better than peanut butter and jelly for me.

I felt stronger than I had felt in some time. I felt clear-minded and with direction. I felt calmer, no matter the situation or how others were acting around me. I was centered and rooted with unwavering confidence. I didn't have all the answers, but my sense of self was high, and I knew I'd figure the rest out. Not knowing the answers or what I would do was calming; I had faith and knew I had the capability, strength, and perseverance to push any boulder up any mountain. Bring. It. On. If you have seen the 1976 movie *Rocky*, this is my proverbial run up the seventy-two stone steps in front of the

Philadelphia Museum of Art to end my morning jog with a dancing jog at the top, fist pumps in the air.

At one point in this journey of several months, one of my closest friends and I were out for coffee and a catching-up conversation, when she said to me, "So, Theresa, what has changed for you? Because you seem happier than I have seen you be in a long time. Did you get a new job? Or win the lotto? What is going on?" I had not changed jobs and certainly had not won the lotto. But, man oh man, things were changing! This was my most significant Edison Moment. Somehow, her comment unlocked the treasure chest, turned on the brightest light, and I became calm and relaxed, filled with love and optimism. Yes! I was happier!

With the small, consistent daily efforts I committed to, I made meaningful changes. I found my purpose in creativity, innovation, and service and anchored to it. Looking back at my journey, I can't even recognize where I started from. I loved many aspects of my job, but it was the environment and people that were not a good match for me and were genuinely changing me, and not for the better. This did not make me a weak, broken, or damaged person. Not all environments or people are good matches. It's okay to acknowledge that. Yes, I could have stayed in that environment and continued to shrink smaller and smaller, transforming into the type of indistinguishable employee that specific area of the company and its leaders seemed to value. But I did not have to choose that path either. I chose a different path, and I'm glad I did!

With my found purpose in creativity and serving others, I continued to frame my perspective, which helped me identify the exact action steps I wanted. Hard work was still to come, but with a sense of purpose that I anchored to, I was energized, strong, and focused. Grit, determination, and perseverance were at all-time highs, and I was ready for the next step: framing my perspective.

Examples of Purpose

- Integrity
- Courage
- Creativity
- Innovation
- Respect
- Honesty
- Communication
- Accountability
- Service
- Growth
- Balance
- Sustainability
- Adaptability
- Adventure
- Challenge
- Contribution
- Humor
- Influence
- Justice
- Equitability
- Love
- Recognition
- Social Justice
- Stability

My Crossroads is _____ .

My Purpose is _____ .

Use the space above to capture the distilled insights and to assist in anchoring you to this purpose. Writing down one's purpose and crossroads can be a transformative strength. You make it concrete through the act of writing. It changes from thoughts and feelings occupying a lot of space in your head, heart, and soul to words on paper, external to you.

This act of writing can be the catalyst, or spark, in beginning to clear space for you to continue the journey as we frame your perspective. Are you ready to see the world from a new perspective?

STEP II
FRAMING PERSPECTIVE

Mantra: "You can observe a lot just by watching." ~Yogi Berra

Framing perspective can often be the most challenging part in navigating a crossroads. It considers other information that may adjust your thinking, feeling, or behavior. It may offer alternative meanings of the context or experience you are navigating. You often begin to see the world from different views. There may be a merry-go-round of feelings and thoughts that can be physically and mentally exhausting and overwhelming. So, prepare for what might feel like a cyclical process ahead, remembering that you are making significant progress with each revolution.

Here is yet another unvarnished truth to start us on this second step toward meaningful change and growth—framing your perspective is likely to get a bit uncomfortable, leaving you vulnerable.

We will discuss strategies for framing perspective and becoming comfortable with being uncomfortable. There are likely actions or habits you already have that you can lean into, reminding you of your inner strengths. There are likely people or examples in your life, too, that can help you remember, clarify, and adopt the perspective needed to navigate your crossroads. Your perspective evolves with you as you grow, change, and learn. It adapts to the present and future contexts while remaining anchored to your purpose. Your experiences shape your perspective. We can find, refine, and forge ahead with a clear perspective by intentionally examining your experiences.

The vast examples and information surrounding us daily can frame and influence perspective. One's perspective can be motivated or challenged when one sees examples around them of goals or aspirations one is working toward but has yet to reach. Societal influences from a digital age and access to technology often invite information overload 24/7. It can be very easy to think you're not doing enough or are missing out on the it-factor that separates you from the rest of the population who are effortlessly having success. This tiny crack of self-doubt or self-blame can quickly expand into a waterfall, increasing the feelings of overwhelmingness and deterring you from your goal(s). Assumptions we make (consciously or not) can also color our perspective.

A crossroads experience can often feel like an onslaught of fluid emotions. You might feel like you're in an uncomfortable, discouraging, depleted state of crisis, and it is taking forever to navigate. Simultaneously, you may still have recurring, sporadic, or planned moments when life feels like an exciting adventure filled with wonder, curiosity, opportunity, and possibility. You may even feel unburdened. How in the world can these two opposing viewpoints be reconciled? In the apt words of Dorothy in *The Wizard of Oz*, "I've a feeling we're not in Kansas anymore."

Entering an uncomfortable crossroads can undoubtedly be akin to being swept up by an unexpected tornado that magically transports you to a Munchkinland without a wicked witch, the shiny red shoes, or a dog named Toto. As you navigate your crossroads (the metaphorical yellow brick road, in this case), you will likely encounter friends and foes along the way, as Dorothy and Toto did on their journey. Ultimately, Dorothy experienced a transformative journey where she considered several perspectives before renewing her inner strength (anchoring to her purpose), leading her to her courageous conviction for meaningful change.

How we each navigate our metaphorical yellow brick road journey directly informs our experience and the efficiency by which we can elevate ourselves to the next level and make a meaningful, long-lasting change. To accomplish this, we lean on the 7 Essential Elements to find our perspective applied to the specific crossroads we are navigating. Following that, we can engage four experiments to make framing your perspective interactive and fun.

The 7 Essential Elements of Perspective

Perspective helps us understand and organize the onslaught of information, feelings, and emotions spinning faster than a revolving door. Perspective allows us to shape our sense of self and helps us identify actionable goals to work toward meaningful change. Perspective helps us ensure we do not stay stuck because we continually move and grow with purpose and intention toward our goals.

> *Mantra: "You gain strength, courage, and confidence by every experience in which you really stop to look fear in the face. You are able to say to yourself, 'I lived through this horror. I can take the next thing that comes along.' " ~Eleanor Roosevelt*

Let's look closer at the 7 Essential Elements to help us frame our perspective. These elements can be considered in any order, and you may even find that some contexts or situations may not call on all 7 Essential Elements to be used.

Essential Elements	The Main Idea	Examples in Practice
Current Self-Assessment	Reflect and identify where you are today in the immediate present. This helps orient you so you do not try to compare older or future versions of yourself. Remember that our experiences shape our perspective, and our perspective is adaptable and flexible to our constantly evolving selves. The *you* that you were last week was great, and the *you* that you are today is better! This view positions us to be in a constant state of growth and learning. We can adapt flexibly and with intention.	Picture yourself in a car, and the crossroads situation is the environment around you, would you more often find yourself . . . A. looking out the back window or rearview mirror, focusing on what you've passed that is now behind you? B. looking out the side windows or somewhere inside the car, now focused on things within your immediate surroundings? C. looking out the front window, gaze locked on what you can see approaching and anticipating what you cannot see ahead? Finally, consider where you are located in the car after you've reflected on A, B & C. Are you in the back seat? Front driver's side? Front passenger's side? Are you in control of the car? Is it a car like I had in drivers ed, allowing full control from both front seats; which then begs the question, is anyone else in the car driving for you right now?

Rank and Organize	This is when we acknowledge the vast amounts of information we receive and need to process in any given moment.	As you think about yourself as the main leading character in the crossroads event, how might you rank the impact of these items from highest to lowest:
	The objective here is to prioritize and categorize the information gleaned from the current self-assessment.	**Self-Esteem:** Do you find that feelings are spilling out everywhere? Do you feel a heightened state of emotions? Do you feel you can control your emotions? Or perhaps some days, does it seem like they might control you?
	It is not about judgment of those details. Rather, this element helps you see a clear starting place based on the way you classify the current information that is most relevant to you right now.	**Self-Concept:** Do you find that negative thoughts about your skills, abilities, or potential are screaming in your head? Is there a deafening "noise" and nonstop self-talk in your head? Does it feel like you have two opposing views battling out the Great Debate on each shoulder, using your ears as their megaphones to be heard?
	This information can (and will likely) change as you refine and grow through the normal process of navigating your crossroads.	**Self-Efficacy:** Do you find that even when you are taking action steps, the intended or desired outcome does not occur time after time? Even if you've accomplished the action in the past (perhaps even more times than you can count), but now for some reason, despite taking what seems to be the same approach, no action or the opposite reaction is happening?
	Self-esteem is driven by our emotions. Self-concept is driven by our thoughts. Self-efficacy is driven by our behaviors.	
	If we picture these three pieces as the sides of a triangle, the dominant element will form the top point of the triangle. This gives us a starting place from which to work on finding and refining our perspective.	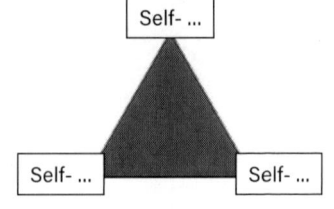
	We can rotate the triangle however we need and may find we do so while finding our perspective.	

Validating Connection to Purpose	This is the first time we directly call upon our purpose.	Earlier I shared an example of a career-related crossroads I experienced when I was able to identify my purpose anchored to creativity and service.
	Intentionally link to the purpose and your "why" identified in Step One.	When I proceeded to find my perspective, I was able to remind myself that no matter how I choose to proceed forward, my action steps would somehow directly anchor to creativity and service.
	This anchor can help to guide and reshape the perspective in the immediate moment as well as how you plan your goals.	
	This is often a milestone moment when the energy starts to build. A destination on the map may start to appear, even if the picture quality is still fuzzy—something is on the map!	This experience I acknowledge I was in the front driver's seat of the car and very much looking out only the front window (Current Self-Assessment). All sights were on the future with little attention paid to the present or the past. I was eager and ready for a new beginning. I was also able to clarify that the leading character for me was self-esteem (Rank and Organize). It was the ping-ponging feelings of anxiety and excitement that were both exhausting me and motivating me. I felt like they were a bit like ping-pong balls though, haphazardly knocking around without a clear direction or goal.
	Often, this is a marker in the process that provides the validation and affirmation that positive and productive change is happening. Even if you know the process is not finished, and there may still be a ways to go, reassurance can be helpful.	When I could pause, and anchor to my purpose, I rechanneled the anxiety and excitement into searching for ways to engage my goals of creativity and service. I did this through not only applying for new jobs that described responsibilities encompassing these elements but also in how I approached the job search process. I thought creatively outside of any normal square box. I identified the functional skills I had gleaned, categorized them by proficiency levels, and then leveraged the career tools I had (AI did not exist at this time) to forge new pathways for myself (Validating Connection to Purpose). This opened up roads for me to traverse industries between clinical counseling, education, government, nonprofit, and healthcare.

Clear the Shelves	During this phase, our objective is to capitalize on the embers of momentum you are generating in preparation for the moment of clarity that is destined to occur.	This can be a challenging element depending upon the type of crossroads situation and each person's readiness and tolerance for change.
	We identify and replace any old perspectives with new perspectives ripe with new language describing our truths.	In this element we are reframing our thoughts, feelings, and behaviors, making space for new possibilities. We are not trying to manipulate, avoid, or deny. We stick to truth and facts. The change happens when we begin seeing and acknowledging other truths beyond what we knew before we reached this point.
	You may find that you're reframing your sense of self or your identity with this element. For example, perhaps you've always identified yourself as a person anyone could come and talk to about their problems even if that was not your job. Now, finding your new perspective, you'd like to establish new boundaries to protect your energy while remaining approachable and available to help others, but not like before.	Let's go back to Ike (President Dwight D. Eisenhower, 34th president of the United States of America), who is considered the catalyst and one of the founders of the American Interstate Highway System. Using the Interstate Highway, we can travel from Boston, MA, to Los Angeles, CA. That may have been a route we've taken in the past that worked well.
		Now, however, after reflecting and learning from our new experiences, and a new purpose we are anchoring to, we can see more than one way to travel across America from the East Coast to the West Coast. We might still have a goal of starting in Boston, MA, and ending in Los Angeles, CA, but *how* we travel with the new possibilities, which we have made room for on the proverbial shelf, has opened up many options. We may even reconsider if California is still the best end destination for us—there are a lot of West Coast destinations that are appealing while remaining anchored to our current purpose.
	Or, perhaps you've always defined your career abilities or career goals as a teacher, but now you are interested in leveraging the problem-solving strengths you have, showcasing those skills and abilities, applying them to computers and data.	
	When we clear the shelves, we make room for new possibilities to be uncovered and considered.	We do not need to choose at this point, but we do open ourselves up to endless brainstorming and possibilities of what could be framed by a new outlook and perspective.

Daily Task Identification	What is the realistic and achievable number of tasks you can balance daily? Identify what these tasks are, noting they may not be identical every day. Take the same amount of time if they recur multiple days a week. Understand this will likely evolve, but start as soon as possible with daily tasks that will connect to the Future Target Goals.	Time to get ready for action. Now that we have started identifying your perspective, finding which feels like the best match, let's add fuel to that fire. Here is how we refine your perspective and reinforce it is the best match for you right now. The Daily Task Identification step is the precursor to short-term goals and then the long-term goals. You create a roadmap for yourself and reverse engineer how you are going to optimize your successful results starting with repeatable and achievable daily tasks. Career crossroads example: The Future Target Long-Term Goal is "I will be employed as a data analyst and remote worker in the technology industry within 6–8 months." The daily tasks may include the following that could be spread across multiple days like mini projects: • Identifying the top five companies you'd like to work at. • Retrieving data analyst position descriptions from those companies to analyze and review. • Cross-examining your current skills against the job description. • Auditing and identifying training and skill development required.

Future Target Short-Term Goals	Identify 1-3 specific goals that are realistic, achievable, and still challenging that can be accomplished within one month, two months, and three months (can go up to six months). The Daily Task Identification will directly help you to successfully fulfill the short-term goals identified.	This is when we push beyond the daily tasks and identify at least one target that can be achieved within 2-6 months. The daily tasks you are completing should directly support this goal. Reaching this goal will directly contribute to the long-term goal you've identified. This can be a good milestone moment to build in a celebratory reward for yourself. I love food, so my celebratory rewards often involve trying a new local restaurant. Returning to our career crossroads example: The Future Target Long-Term Goal is "I will be employed as a data analyst and remote worker in the technology industry within 6-8 months." The Future Target Short-Term Goals may include the following that could be spread across the 2-6 months: • Make a plan to complete the upskilling needed (each skill has its own deadline for completion). • Update resume (completed by month four). • Apply for jobs (completed by month six).
Future Target Long-Term Goals	Identify one specific goal that is your destination, even if in concept. The short-term goals will directly help you to successfully fulfill this identified long-term target.	For example, you might have a Future Target Long-Term Goal that is "I will be employed as a data analyst and remote worker in the technology industry within 6-8 months."

Mantra: "Setting goals is the first step in turning the invisible into the visible." ~Tony Robbins

As we clarify and frame our perspective, we must be prepared to feel vulnerable and uncomfortable. This step makes us stop and question, assess, and consider aspects of ourselves and how we make meaning of the contextual situations around us. It is very common to float between analyzing past experiences and predicting future experiences during this step and to skip over what is happening in the present moment. Rushing through it is ubiquitous because the heightened levels of vulnerability can be uncomfortable.

In my personal experience, this step to clarify and frame perspective is when I am most challenged. When I was in high school and applying to colleges in the 1990s, like my friends, we all applied to a small handful. I was an average student in my school, usually on the honor roll, hovering around a B+ or an A- for my overall grades. I took AP classes in math, English, and foreign language, participated in multiple seasons of school sports, and was a part of some after-school clubs. I also held a part-time job when I could get my work papers at sixteen.

While I enjoyed school and the overall learning process, test-taking was not an area I excelled at in school. I knew the information but translating it to a pencil-and-paper test did not always indicate I knew the material. Standardized tests, like the SATs, were my nemesis. When the college decision letters started arriving in the fall of my senior year, I recall my friends receiving acceptance letters from multiple schools. They had the opportunity to choose from many invitations, and their crossroads became which interested school to choose from.

My experience, however, was different. I received several rejection letters citing my SAT scores or overall GPA were lower than the average student profile they were seeking. I was applying to mostly public state schools that, based on their student profiles and the programs the admissions representatives shared, would be a good match. The in-state tuition discount was a primary motivator; even in the early 1990s, paying for college was expensive, although I know those prices do not compare to the current costs of today.

I was not reaching for the stars with the schools I was interested in. I did not apply to the top Ivy League schools. In addition to straight rejections, I received some waitlist letters that, after holding out hope for a few more months, were updated to rejections, too. The only acceptance letter I received was from one local-area state school I applied to.

I had applied to this school, not expecting to rely on that school as my only option. I expected to be like my friends—to be "burdened" by the countless opportunities in front of me to choose where to go to school. Instead, it seemed the decision had been made for me. I was going to the local state school.

The day this realization hit me, I felt like a pack of elephants had trampled me. I remember feeling sorry for myself, letting the negative language drown my self-concept. The thoughts swimming through my head would criticize how I was not smart enough to be accepted anywhere else, and it was obvious to everyone, as evidenced by the wallpaper of rejection letters I received. I wrapped myself in a blanket of shame, blame, and self-pity.

One day, not long after receiving the acceptance letter to the local school, my dad came into the room and saw my tear-stained cheeks. He sat beside me calmly. "Theresa, why are you so upset?" he asked with concern and love. I explained to him my reasoning, which, in my head, tainted by all of the negativity, seemed to be wholly rational and obvious. He listened openly and without judgment. He considered the points I was making, even though I am confident he could see through the weak arguments I was putting up. When he spoke, he said, "Theresa, you do have a choice.

You can choose to go to this school or not. A decision has not been made for you. You still need to make a decision."

My perspective had been twisted in knots from the negativity. In an instant, my dad offered me a different viewpoint to consider. He helped me clear my shelves and create space for a new possibility to consider. This allowed me to quiet the negative voices distracting my self-concept and self-esteem.

Yes! I did have a choice!

I had yet to learn how many options were ready and waiting for me to step up and direct my future in unimaginable ways. I was not a victim, even though it felt that way before framing my perspective. I am fortunate to be blessed with the best dad ever. The impact his few words and presence had on my formative seventeen-year-old self in that moment was the catalyst for the decades after. Sometimes, it only takes a moment and a few words to alter a person's life trajectory.

When we are at a crossroads, it is very common that we compare ourselves to others. I compared myself to my friends and made many assumptions about their experiences. This is a normal response for anyone at a crossroads and trying to make sense of the situation, regardless of their age.

I had shifted my focus and framed my perspective by comparing myself only to what was happening to my friends. What schools were they getting into, what number of schools offered them enrollment, etc.. I had forgotten my purpose, the reason why I was focused on attending university in the first place. Without my purpose to anchor to, I had gone adrift, lost at sea, disoriented at which direction was true north because I could not see the sun through the veil of gray, foggy clouds. My dad helped remind me that if I remembered why I was interested in attending university (finding my purpose), I could find my way across the sea to my destination (framing my perspective). At this point in my life, my purpose was anchored to adventure and accountability.

I knew I wanted to have a career built upon a foundation of psychology, helping as many people as possible, but I had yet to identify a specific role or job. I knew this local state school had a few brilliant faculty members engaged in areas of research I found very interesting. I also learned the school's undergraduate and graduate programs offered opportunities for applied internships and some scholarships and tuition assistance opportunities. I was familiar with the local area and had a driver's license and a car to get around and take advantage of these possibilities because I had been working and saving money.

It didn't stop there. I discovered at this university, I could set my schedule, allowing me to keep my existing part-time job (or get a new one, which happened in the fall semester of my freshman year) while still going to school full-time and engaging in an internship. My friends who attended other universities had to complete a prescribed first-year curriculum that required a presence on campus five days a week with courses spread throughout full days with large blocks of open time. They could not work during their first year due to schedule restrictions, except for small approved on-campus work-study positions. The perspective was changing dramatically!

I learned of a comprehensive study-abroad option offered at the university I was accepted to, which I took advantage of during my junior year. I had never entertained the idea of traveling to Europe because, growing up, that was never a realistic financial expense in my family. I never felt without, but now, I could travel and study at a university in another country, continue earning college credits, and live with a host family that doesn't speak English for a full-semester immersion experience! This is my life? What?

How could a student who was rejected by every university she applied to except for one have so many opportunities to choose to engage in? Perspective and Purpose. Thank you, Dad, for being the catalyst to get this started for me!

By framing my perspective, anchored to my purpose of accountability and adventure, I then saw the endless choices and opportunities available for my future. The negative inward language dissipated, replaced by excitement, renewed confidence, and a desire to accomplish everything available to me. I was no longer driven by comparing myself to my friends or others around me.

My energy source was a rapidly building internal desire to learn and to be a sponge, soaking up as much as possible. How could I take advantage of as much as possible while I was at the university? That became a driving question. My perspective shifted and invited the space for my passion to be discovered.

> Mantra: "Once you replace negative thoughts with positive ones, you'll start having positive results." ~Willie Nelson

An easy way to see your progress concretely, as you clarify and frame your perspective, is by maintaining a running list of daily accomplishments. At the end of every week, fill in any helpful details or contexts you may have missed when you reflect on this list. You can keep this in a Word document on your computer or in a notebook, but set it up and diligently add to it throughout this transitional crossroads. This concrete resource of all you are doing and have accomplished is a terrific reminder that you are *not* stuck in the same place. Change *is* happening, daily and weekly. While there may appear to be similarities week after week (focus on applying for jobs), the crossroads and associated experiences you are navigating now are changing with every effort you make.

Change happens all around us every day. It may not always be crystal clear, but you change every day. You grow, learn, think about something from a new perspective, or add new knowledge, enhancing your lived experiences.

Perspective is a vital tool for understanding contextual situations and experiences. Perspective is influenced and informed by you. Some of us may be hardwired in a way that makes flexible perspectives and adapting to change more innate; others of us may need to practice and develop this skill more often. It is undoubtedly achievable for any person who puts forth the effort.

Let's apply the idea of challenging and learning more about our perspective through experiments. If you accept it, your mission is to remain open to the possibilities of each of these experiments. Yes, most of them are silly and I do hope you find yourself laughing, as humor and joy are powerhouses to accelerate the introspective process required in finding and refining our perspective. Start with Experiment #1, or be daring and start with Experiment #4. Hop around or go in order. You choose! I ask that you remain open to all possible insights and watch for your unique Edison Moments. Sometimes, you only need one to find what you are looking for; other times, you need all of them.

Experiment #1: Making Lemonade from Lemons

Mantra: "All that is gold does not glitter, / Not all those who wander are lost; / The old that is strong does not wither, / Deep roots are not reached by the frost." ~J. R. R. Tolkien

When life seems to be throwing lemons at you, many people say, "Well, make lemonade!" as if it's just that easy. But here is the secret: You don't need to make a simple syrup of dissolved sugar and water to sweeten a situation, like you do when making that sweet and tart, citrusy drink from scratch. It's all about perspective.

Ready for a simple yet powerful experiment? Here's a small task you can do in one week, centered on how you wake up to start your day, to demonstrate the power of perspective. I'll even give you three variations of how to approach this experiment. For the recovering perfectionists and overachievers reading, it's okay to apply all three options simultaneously. You do you! It is also okay to pick one and start there. Are you ready to see a shift in your mindset and perspective?

Choose and implement one (or more) of the options below every day for seven consecutive days. Yes, including weekends. Yes, even if you're on vacation or traveling for work. Yes, even if you've had a busy day or long stretch this week. Starting tomorrow morning, let's get after it. Day 1 tomorrow, and proceed for the following six days. Yes, you can!

> **Option A:** It's time to get up. To start, sit up in bed, ideally; although, if you promise not to fall back asleep, you can do this while lying in bed. Grab that cell phone or smartwatch if you need to set a timer to ensure you hold it for the entire duration.

Your task: Each morning for thirty seconds, as soon as you turn off that alarm and before you get out of bed, hold a smile.

That's it. Even if you need to start with a slight grin, tomorrow on Day 1, and eventually build to a smile to let those pearly whites shine by Day 7, that will work. Thirty seconds is all I ask of you to give this variation a try.

Option B: Preplan a music playlist. It's time to get up. To start, turn on your playlist before your feet touch the floor or as you get out of bed. This playlist only needs to be around fifteen minutes long. Choose music with upbeat tempos encouraging you to bust out into a spontaneous dance party before you've even brushed your teeth or had a cup of coffee. Edit your playlist at any time! Now, you don't need to have a spontaneous dance party, but I also won't discourage it for those feeling spicy on a given morning.

Your task: Each morning, after turning off your alarm and before you get out of bed or while you're getting out of bed, listen to at least fifteen minutes of upbeat music from your playlist.

If your partner (or your family pet) would be less than thrilled to have music playing when you get up, pop in the AirPods or earbuds and jam out. I've found this to work best with my usual morning routine and to let the music play on my cell phone as I get out of bed (even if my sassy pit bull Maze gives me an unimpressed look at the noise I'm creating while she's still sleeping). Song one starts while I'm making my bed. By the time song two comes on, I'm getting dressed for the gym or brushing my teeth. By the time song three comes on, I'm dancing down the hallway of my house to gather my stuff to head to the gym. If it's a day I'm not starting at the gym, I may have the music playing while I'm getting the coffee pot started and showering. The capability to listen to music through a cell phone is so convenient.

Songs I have on my morning playlist currently:

- "Roll It (Main)" by Shontelle
- "Dance Hall Days" by Wang Chung
- "Súbeme la Radio" by Enrique Iglesias
- "Everyone C'mon" by The New Black Tea
- "Born For This" by The Score
- "Let's Get It Started" by The Black Eyed Peas
- "Any Way You Want It" by Journey
- "Crazy Train" by Ozzy Osbourne
- "Happy" by Pharrell Williams

If none of these songs tap into your creative juices, consider a streaming service dedicated to music, and use the Search function to discover upbeat options aligned with your taste.

Option C: It's time to get up. To start, make your bed as soon as you get up. What if I don't sleep alone and my partner is still sleeping when I get up? Make your side of the bed. Even if your partner pulls those covers or sheets again and snuggles with your pillow, you went through those steps, and it will make a difference in your day. For those who sleep alone, make that bed completely.

Your task: Make your bed as soon as you get out of it (or at least your side of the bed). The estimated total time needed is less than one minute.

While bedmaking is something I was forced to do as a kid, I wasn't paying attention to the subtle yet positive impacts that brief action was having. Decades later, I read the book by Admiral William H. McRaven, aptly named *Make Your Bed*. Now, I get it. Admiral McRaven shared ten principles he learned while completing US Navy SEALs training that helped him navigate the challenges and obstacles this program, designed to create superhuman badass operators, threw his way daily. These men and women are among the elite special forces in the US military and do not have lemons thrown at them like you or me. Oh, no, they have tons of pomelos coming their way, and they navigate them with surgical precision. Fun fact—for those wondering what a pomelo is, it is considered the largest citrus fruit, typically around ten inches in diameter. It is native to Asia and Malaysia and has a taste similar to that of grapefruit. Since I started a citrus analogy earlier, I thought I'd keep that consistent here. You can also find a quick summary of the ten principles Admiral McRaven describes in his book on YouTube, or better yet, read the book! This topic was the foundation of a commencement address he gave at the University of Texas at Austin on May 17, 2014.

Let's recap—you can choose one (or more) of the three options above to fit into your unique schedule and lifestyle. Starting tomorrow as Day 1 and continuing for six consecutive days you will engage in an experiment centered around how you start your day as soon as your alarm goes off.

Option A requires thirty seconds daily. Option B requires approximately fifteen minutes daily, and you can be doing other things simultaneously. Option C requires less than one minute daily. I know you have the time to give this a try. What have you got to lose?

After the seven days have elapsed, check in with yourself and how you're feeling. Pay attention and identify common thoughts, feelings, and behaviors. The small changes we make to our daily routines, especially when they influence how we start and approach each day, have a broader impact. Your perspective selectively identifies positive interpretations and opportunities. It filters into a strength-based perspective. You will remember the playful and happy spirit within you, even if the responsibilities and situations you navigate during the day may tamp those traits down.

Mantra: "Progress is impossible without change, and those who cannot change their minds cannot change anything." ~George Bernard Shaw

Experiment #2: Riding the (Tidal) Wave of Negativity to the Shore

Mantra: There will always be people who do not see or care to see your worth. Don't let yourself be among that group of people.

As discussed earlier when we were finding purpose, negativity can be powerful and permeate thoughts, emotions, and behaviors. We can receive negativity from within and from those around us. This experiment is designed to help us clarify the location(s) of our negative source(s) and then devise an action plan to mitigate it as we overpower the negativity with positive gratitude.

The process of identifying and devising action plans can feel like riding a tidal wave. There is a fluidity to the process that can simultaneously be overwhelming, seemingly never-ending, strong, and terrifying. This is normal. So, let's ride this wave to the shore together.

First, identify the location of your negative tidal wave. Most commonly, this can be from one of two sources: internal negativity, stemming from your self-worth, or external negativity, stemming from others or influenced by the environment around you. It can also be true that both are active sources. Typically, one is the catalyst we want to identify in starting this process.

A "devil and angel" argument is one common sign of internal negativity. A situation or experience will occur (it need not stem from anything rational), and your go-to reaction will be inward blame, self-directed put-downs, or otherwise admonishing yourself with words spoken aloud, written down, or merely as thoughts in your head. You may or may not have a rebuttal, as if your angel side was trying to counterargue the point. Picture images of a courtroom and arguments before a judge—Who will win?

When we catch ourselves having these dichotomous thoughts and internal debates, we are often questioning and overthinking. These thoughts can quickly build momentum. The spiral effect gains so much energy it becomes hard to control, leaving us helpless and overwhelmed. Remember that you are stronger than you think in those moments.

Acknowledge, respect, and move on from those thoughts. You had the thoughts, okay. You can control the debate, even if it didn't feel like you could moments earlier. You deserve grace and forgiveness. Every human has these moments. The frequency of how often they occur and how we navigate through them can be an empowering difference among us.

Often, one way to break the cycle is to ask yourself honestly, "Would I just say the same words in the same tone with the same [intentions / judgments / accusations] to . . . ?" Finish this sentence by identifying one of the most influential people in your life right now. A child, a partner, a parent, a sibling, a best friend, a roommate. You choose who is the best person to imagine at that moment.

When I ask myself this question and every time I use this question when working with a client or a student, I have yet to hear "I wouldn't change a thing I said" or "I wouldn't change a thing I thought."

We can be incredibly cruel, disparaging, and demanding toward ourselves when we are in the throws of an internal entropic battle. The power of the internal negative tidal wave is no joke when you're in the midst of it. This state of being feels real in the moment, without question. It can even begin to feel rational. The negative thoughts are loud, vicious, and with powerful conviction that can be crippling to our self-esteem, self-confidence, and self-worth.

You can doubt and question your value, your purpose, and your trust in yourself to make reasonable and healthy decisions, and still continue: "Why bother trying anymore? It's not happening for me." "I'm just not smart enough." "I'll never get the job or get into the school I have been trying for." "The fact that I keep failing is a sign my time is up, regardless that I had done well up to this point."

Ask yourself: "Would I say any of those comments to one of the most important or influential people in my life? Would I ever say those things to my partner or my family? *No!* Then why would it ever be acceptable to say those things to myself?" The answer is that it is not.

So, how do we start making a change when we are aware of the ongoing negative tidal wave? How do we combat the blossoming effect even one ounce of negativity can have on our mind, body, and spirit?

Have you ever been driving to work or running errands and someone else cuts you off or drives their car in a less-than-safe manner for you and others around you? Have you also, in these instances, had an uncontrolled urge to yell expletives to that stranger who would likely never hear those words you say? Many of us can relate to this type of situation. Many of us are emboldened to express our unfiltered thoughts and feelings, instantly capitalizing on the in-the-moment experience. Perhaps you feel an immediate sense of validation after expressing your thoughts and feelings from within the safety of your own car because the person deserved it, whatever "it" may be. Now, I ask you, how do you typically feel immediately after unleashing that rage?

Often, when I've worked with clients navigating their negative tidal wave, the immediate reaction to follow is a wash of more negativity by way of guilt or disappointment in themselves for overreacting or letting something or someone else get to them. Negative reactions influence and breed more negativity. Sometimes, one bad-driver experience while commuting to work can color the rest of the morning, or even the entire day, leaving a sour or bitter taste in your mouth. It is important to recognize and distinguish between when we are *reacting* (fueling negativity) and when we are *taking action* (fueling positivity).

When you are reacting, you might experience changes in your mood, irritability or a desire to further withdraw from people or activities. You may decline invitations with friends, family, or new colleagues to socialize or engage. Depression, uncomfortable feelings of vulnerability and hypersensitivity, shame, and self-doubt are all indicators you might be surfing a negative tidal wave. You may also see signs in your sleep habits and an overall decline in the quality of your sleep, feeling tired, fatigued, or lethargic. Thinking clearly and having the energy to complete tasks, even the most common among them, may be harder than you remember them being before.

Yes, this negativity is very similar to the negativity that can weigh you down and block your progress when searching for your purpose. Negativity can be very one-dimensional. Once we become practiced at recognizing how negativity tries to weigh us down and stunt our progress, we can begin to recognize it and defuse it proactively. Then we can retain more of our energy and redirect it toward productive efforts in guiding change and growth.

People need the energy to explore options, to clarify and frame their perspectives when navigating a crossroads. Mental fortitude, flexibility, and strength to overcome days that feel like seas of never-ending setbacks and rejections demand energy. Strategies to see, feel, and recognize adverse actions, feelings, and thoughts and then tamp down their negative impacts are essential.

> *Mantra: Negative thoughts will always try to come in, but they do not come from within.*

You are worthy of employment if you receive a rejection email from a job you applied to. You are worthy of love and a healthy, safe relationship with a partner, even if your marriage or relationship with another person has just ended. A positive psychological shift occurs when you change your mindset. It starts by thinking, and then believing the context is true. You control how you show up. Your beliefs about yourself and your values will influence your perspective.

Next, let's turn to our immediate network of people to accomplish two things. First, it provides us with the information to know if we have any external negativity sources, and second, it confirms who the people are that we need in our essential network.

The essential network is comprised of around five to seven people, or contributors, who are your greatest sources of support, positivity, and unlimited encouragement in the specific situation you are navigating. Sometimes, this essential network remains constant across contexts and crossroads. Other times, the network shifts. For example, I have different essential network contributors for my career-related crossroads than my personal- and family-related crossroads. There might be individual people who traverse networks.

Your essential network contributors are there to pick you up, not put you down. They are not there to do the hard work for you but to support and remind you that you are never alone. They empower you to be the best version of yourself, even if you are still trying to discover that version. They are flexible and adaptable as you grow, evolve, and learn along your life's journey, celebrating with you and supporting you through the challenges. They are sources of empathy, joy, love, courage, and curiosity, reminding you of your gifts and unique talents that make you your best self. You feel happier, lighter, and more positive after spending time or speaking with them, even if it's about complex or difficult topics.

Negative sources can be environments, things or external factors, or people. In this context, let's zero in on the negative source contributors to understand the opposite of an essential network contributor. Negative source contributors are the people who make comments or take actions that invoke in you unproductive overthinking and questioning. They illicit doubt, uncertainty, and anxiety. They make you question your value and aptitude, even if you know the facts don't support that view. If presented with a glass, a negative source contributor may immediately say it's half empty. You may be able to distance yourself from negative source contributors in some situations; other times, they may linger and be unmoving.

I had a career experience once when the supervisor of the area where I worked was a negative source contributor for my personal experience. Other coworkers that shared unsolicited comments described their experiences with this supervisor similarly. This negative source contributor conveyed daily an outlook on life and work rooted in negativity. They cultivated, with intense precision, a team and area of the company based on reactivity, chaos, conflict, and unproductive micromanagement. There was no trust among the team members and no transparency. Team members who one-up others were praised publicly in large group meetings for performances well done. Team members who did not engage in these behaviors were minimized, dismissed, or somehow called out, often creating a sense of embarrassment. It sent the message that negative behavior would be rewarded over true, honest teamwork and collaboration.

This, for me, was a negative tidal wave environment, and for a period of time, I was not able to distance myself from it, as I did not have another job lined up. I had to engage in that environment if I wanted to continue receiving my paycheck. My strategy was to lean on my essential network contributors, which included some individuals who also worked within the same organization, two on the same team, living alongside this experience with me. The rest of my essential network was comprised of family and friends.

My essential network kept me focused on a perspective true to my authentic self, regardless of the negative comments or actions the supervisor or other members of that team, acting on the supervisor's behalf, threw at me. I navigated through the negative tidal wave, not by confrontation, aggression, or by matching the negativity projected at me. Instead, I successfully navigated this negative tidal wave by connecting with my essential network contributors, fueling my positive and authentic self. This critical group of people supported me to let the best version of myself shine brightly regardless of the challenging context I was experiencing at that time. Without my essential network, I would have lived in a survival state with heightened defensiveness, irritability, and a sense of walking on eggshells every day I went to work. I would have needed to change who I was at my core to remain in that environment. My essential network contributors helped me to find the strength and courage, to see a different future for myself, and to make a plan accordingly.

The outcome of the essential network support was my ability to show up to work, see opportunities, be positive, and be productive daily, even in the face of the swirls of negativity in that team and area. I accomplished my work and responsibilities by delivering high-quality results. I did not let the negative environment or people around me become my perspective. I leaned on my essential network contributors anytime I needed to, continued to practice my box breathing and inward gratitude (anchoring to my purpose), and framed my perspective, staying true to my authentic self. It did not take long before I could see new job opportunities worth transitioning into. The other two members of my essential network discovered new career opportunities too.

> *Mantra: Pay attention to the environment and people around you; remember, salt and sugar look the same.*

Let's identify your essential network and your energy sources.

First, reflect on your current crossroads experience and identify the five to seven people you spend the most time with or are the most influential or impactful in your daily life. You can contextualize this if needed. For example, if your crossroads is career-related, then filter your answer to identify the top five to seven people who are most influential or impactful to your career and current work situation. If the crossroads is personal or about your family, filter from that lens. Write down those names in any order and make a list.

Next, review this list and reflect on your interactions with each person noted. Could any of them be negative source contributors? Indicating someone as a negative source means they do not bring you up or support you positively and healthily for this crossroads. It does not mean they can't be an essential network contributor in other crossroads of your life. Instead, it indicates, for this specific crossroads, they are not a good match or source of strength for you. A close friend of mine would put her mother as a negative source for any crossroads related to her romantic relationships, but she will have her mother as an essential network contributor if the topic is a career-related crossroads. Some people are better matches to support and navigate different issues in your life, and that's okay to acknowledge.

Let's identify who the essential network contributors are on that list. Put a star next to the names of the key contenders for your essential network based on the same current crossroads situation. Focusing only on the names starred, broaden your considerations of the names on the list. What do these people have in common as they affect your life? How do they help and support you? How do they help you to bring out the best version of yourself? How do they empower you to continue growing, evolving, and exploring your unique journey in life? How do they react in times of difficulty and vulnerability that you experience as a normal human being?

Mantra: "Surround yourself with only people who are going to lift you higher." ~Oprah Winfrey

The answers to these questions will identify key traits, actions, and characteristics you respond positively to. These outcomes are what you can concretely offer to your essential network contributors when they ask, "How can I help?" Your feedback can identify one or more of these answers to optimize your experience and provide them with clarity on how to be most effective as the essential network contributors support you.

We can amplify our experiences when we align to a growth mindset anchored to our beliefs, values, purpose, and perspective. We can lean on our essential network to help us remain committed and disciplined in this outlook and to support us along the way.

Mantra: "Stay away from negative people, they have a problem for every solution." ~Albert Einstein

Experiment #3: Learning a New Language

Let's face it, life seems to pick up speed with every passing year. It's as if each birthday adds a turbo speed boost hidden in the birthday cake. Our time on earth is limited, and we have the opportunity to make the most of it. This, however, does not mean overburdening and overcommitting ourselves is helpful or productive. A balance is essential and can be challenging to establish or maintain, given how fast-paced our global society has become.

The language we use in everyday conversations often provides a clue about our current state of balance. Listening for keywords that hold positive or negative charges can indicate whether someone is likely feeling balanced or imbalanced.

If we listen for the frequency we hear these important keywords within their contexts, we can identify a helpful starting point for action. These keywords can become a part of our internal self-dialogue. They can be words we say to ourselves without awareness when feeling stressed or imbalanced. If left unaddressed, they can also permeate our connections and conversations with others.

There can be a disconnect between how someone thinks they are presenting themselves and the keywords they often use, especially if the person is struggling. Several clients I've worked with have shared a desire to keep the struggles and stressful moments to themselves so as not to burden anyone in their essential network or those they love. They try to give the impression that everything is okay so those they care about will not worry. This is a normal reaction and desire, for many people, to protect others. It is also a way to avoid dealing with the discomfort within. This seemingly benevolent outward action can often create tumultuous challenges for someone already navigating a crossroads!

I've discovered that by listening and increasing our awareness of fourteen specific keywords and phrases, we can more efficiently mitigate and redirect energy for everyone involved. Unsurprisingly, the negatively charged keywords and phrases chip away at self-confidence and self-esteem and challenge one's clarity of purpose. Negatively charged keywords and phrases can cloud the path ahead, sometimes to the point of feeling entirely engulfed by a blanket of fog.

Conversely, the positively charged keywords and phrases enhance and strengthen confidence and self-esteem and affirm purpose, refining the pathways (yes, plural!) forward. With clarity comes the ability to see and distinguish the *many* opportunities already in front of you right now! It can be incredibly challenging to trust that there is even one opportunity before you when navigating a crossroads.

I know I've experienced that moment, not having the confidence in even one opportunity to show itself when navigating a romantic-relationship crossroads. I reached a point where I questioned if my partner and I still shared core values in supporting our individual growth as people and our collective growth as partners. Was there still a future for us, or had we forged different paths for our future without realizing it? When I looked at my language patterns, most often used regardless of who I was speaking with, I noticed that I used the seven negatively charged keywords and phrases several times daily. I used three of the positively charged keywords and phrases perhaps once or twice a week. The imbalance was profound when I looked at the basic frequency data. Major Edison Moment!

Even as you read this book, not knowing what your current crossroads situation is, I know you have several opportunities available and in front of you this very second that can enhance and strengthen your life and its purpose—Can you see them? Or could those opportunities be masked by a veil of negative keywords and phrases waiting for you to acknowledge their negative presence and to act?

Here's how we can increase our awareness in listening for keywords. I've identified seven negatively charged keywords and phrases and seven positively charged keywords and phrases. There are three simple steps to learning this new language. The best part is you can use this approach in almost any relationship or connection. This skill set can help you understand how to effectively engage with friends, neighbors, colleagues, or supervisors at work, family members, partners, and more.

Negatively Charged Keywords	Positively Charged Keywords
1. Just	1. And
2. But	2. Yes
3. I Can't	3. Absolutely
4. I Won't	4. I Can
5. I Shouldn't	5. I Will
6. No	6. I Must
7. I'm Not Sure	7. Let Me Confirm (within 24 hours)

Mantra: "When you're surrounded by people who share a passionate commitment around a common purpose, anything is possible." ~Howard Schultz

Step 1: Identify and Observe

Our goal, as we seek to identify and observe, is a neutral effort without judgment to gather information and to objectively collect data to disentangle the thoughts and emotions from the behaviors.

Mantra: "Today, I will do what others won't so tomorrow I can accomplish what others can't." ~Jerry Rice

An easy way to start is with a log. Create a simple table in a Word or Excel document or other word processor or spreadsheet editor. A notebook to keep a hard copy is another option.

Log as much or as little as you are able and comfortable doing. That's it. No analysis. No interpretation. Gather information without judgment.

When I work with clients engaging in this exercise for the first time, our starting point is a basic tally system—if they are aware of or observe the use of the word on the list, they mark a tally. At the end of each day, they total the tallies.

Those who love data collection can also capture the time of day, their location, or who they are with. Gathering contextual data about the use of keywords may also be helpful in Step 2.

Step 2: Learning and Understanding

In this step, our goal is to use the information we've gathered from Step 1 to identify patterns, make inferences, and seek to understand the underlying factors contributing to using those keywords. The depth of this exploration and analysis will vary based on the gathered data.

> Mantra: "Great minds discuss ideas; average minds discuss events; small minds discuss people." ~Eleanor Roosevelt

During these moments of reflection, it is helpful to consider and identify whether the negative language is internalized as a reflection of you (negative language you are generating and pointing inward and self-sabotaging) or externalized and you are projecting that negative language onto others or situations. One of the most common ways of externalizing negative language is gossiping, bullying, and spreading rumors about others. Be a great mind and explore your ideas to guide your purposeful change.

It is helpful to continue writing down reactions, thoughts, and insights. You may lean on members of your essential network to discuss your ideas. There is also no time limit; each person derives meaning and deeper understanding from their own unique experiences when they are ready. Sometimes, we need time to process and digest all of the information.

Step 3: Purposeful Change

The objective in this final step is to identify and take one small action step toward purposeful change that will, eventually, quell or remove negative language and replace that space with positive language. This action step can be as small as selecting one of the positive words and purposefully working to use that word instead of its counterpart. For this combination I recommend starting with "and" and "but."

> Mantra: "If you do not change direction, you may end up where you are heading." ~Lao Tzu

Many people use "but" in conversation and are unaware of how frequently it is used. Contextually, it signifies a reason to pause, delay, wait, or otherwise not take immediate action. The word *but* often represents an obstacle. For example, when invited by friends for coffee, saying, "I'd love to meet you, *but* I have such a busy day, and I don't think I can." Or, when you find an advertised job posting that excites you, "I would be perfect for this job, *but* they have qualifications listed on this posting I don't have experience in" or "I don't have the same certification they are asking, so I guess I won't apply." Navigating crossroads is rarely easy. Typically, at least one challenge or conflict, small or large, will reveal itself as a necessary obstacle to overcome. We do not need to add to the challenge or complexity of a challenge by using keywords that are counterproductive to our growth, purposeful change, and future success.

> Mantra: "Obstacles don't have to stop you. If you run into a wall, don't turn around and give up. Figure out how to climb it, go through it, or work around it." ~Michael Jordan

If we replace "but" with "and," we begin to think, feel, and behave differently. Let's revisit those two examples above. Friends invited for coffee might say, "I'd love to meet you, *and* I have such a busy day that I can stop in to grab a coffee and visit for ten to fifteen minutes this time." Or, the advertised job where instead you say or think "I would be perfect for this job, *and* they have qualifications listed on this posting that I don't have experience in, which I know I will pick up quickly because I do have a certification from a related agency and the majority of the skills, experience, and knowledge they are seeking. I need to get my application in today!"

A seemingly small change with a three-letter keyword can have a big impact, and it only needs to take you three small steps. Awareness of when you use the word *but* can be your first small action. Awareness of the contexts when it is used to delay or stall action, illustrating an obstacle, can be your second small action. Finally, intentionally replacing *but* with *and* can be your third small action. You can also choose different keywords from the list to follow a similar approach.

Remember, it may seem awkward at first. Give yourself grace as you begin to implement this small action. Stick with it, and you will start to see firsthand how one small action can have a larger impact on your thoughts, feelings, and behaviors.

We can grow from our challenges and obstacles. True, life is not always fair; others will have experiences or outcomes you want for yourself. Sometimes, life seems equitable, and other times, less so. No matter what, we can each choose how we interpret and make meaning from each situation. It can add value or add stress to your life; you control how you choose to understand each situation.

I want you to have an abundance of value-added experiences throughout your life. It is attainable for every person with intentional effort. The good news is that small actions can help to reach this goal, so there is no reason to delay getting started! Approach each challenge as a competitor for *your* life. Go for the Gold and the proverbial win in your life by optimizing your use of positively charged keywords. This mindset and perspective can help you have an impact and remain anchored to your purpose.

> Mantra: "The last of one's freedoms is to choose one's attitude in any given circumstance." ~Viktor Frankl

Experiment #4: Basic Math for Everyone

Yes, in Step One, we briefly detoured into the world of physics while we were finding our purpose. Now, while we frame our perspective, let's explore a quick math lesson everyone can benefit from. Let's zero in on the four foundational functions: addition, subtraction, multiplication, and division. This is a practical exercise that invites a variety of adaptations.

Often, I use this exercise when exploring the contextual environments I am a part of or working with clients who are exploring new environments or situations. I have worked with some clients who have found it best to apply this math exercise as they consider the people in their lives. This application can also link to our earlier experiment of helping to identify your essential network contributors and negative source contributors. Consider which variation may be best for you based on the crossroads you see right now and try it.

Math Function	Key Elements	Questions to Ask Yourself
Addition	<ul><li>enhancing, strengthening, or contributing value or positivity</li><li>demonstrated in overt and concrete behavioral actions, or through characteristics or traits influencing you and/or your environment</li><li>considered a positive element</li></ul>	What individuals are adding value to my life right now? What experiences are adding value to my life right now? What behaviors, habits, or routines am I doing that now add value?
Subtraction	<ul><li>not considered a positive element or adding meaningful value</li><li>draining, minimizing, dismissing, or admonishing value</li><li>consuming larger amounts of time, energy, or resources to a level that might be considered wasteful part or all of the time</li></ul>	What individuals are demanding or taking my energy? What behaviors, habits, or routines am I doing that now are not adding value? What experiences are draining my energy at an unusually fast rate compared to other areas of my life? Note: This does not mean the behaviors are necessarily harmful. We are identifying them as not adding meaningful value. For example, stopping for a delicious $5.95 cup of fancy coffee at my local coffee shop every morning on my way to work is a nice treat and a tasty way to start my day. Still, this is an excellent example of a non-value-added expense. It is a literal expense in money and time. This stop requires me to leave my house earlier than usual and rush more if the lines are long on any given morning. If I end up getting stuck in a longer line, or traffic gets backed up on the highway or in town as I get closer to work, I've added even more stress to my morning. Then the question becomes How long will it take to reset myself from a stressful starting day to a "normal" day?

			It is always a gamble how much stress will be added to any given morning. I can always expect time and money expenses any morning I choose to add this stop. Alternatively, I could have a cup of coffee at home while I'm getting ready for my day, saving money and optimizing time while still getting the morning boost of caffeine. The coffee habit of stopping and purchasing fancy and tasty coffee from my local coffee shop is not harmful, but it subtracts value.
Multiplication	<ul><li>intensifying or expanding quickly while adding, enhancing, strengthening, or contributing value</li><li>considered a positive element</li><li>often considered the accelerated version of "addition"</li></ul>		What feels like it quickly impacts and magnifies positivity, strength, or empowerment for you? This might be a person who lifts your spirits anytime you're around them. This might be an activity, environment, or place that reenergizes you or suddenly makes you feel happier. An example I experience is the addictive rush of neurochemicals as the natural byproduct of a good workout. Sixty total minutes at the gym and I'm a renewed woman. And sometimes the workouts need only be fifteen minutes to reset me. A go-to for me when at work is to step outside. Admittedly, this has a stronger effect when the sun is shining, but I do recharge quickly on a rainy or snowy day. Fresh air for ten minutes can often bring me back to life quickly. Other examples might be taking time to walk, read, meditate, cook, be with your family pet, play with your kids, engage in a hobby you and your partner love doing together, or catch up on your backlog of saved shows on your favorite streaming service.

Division	<ul><li>not considered a positive element</li><li>often considered the accelerated version of "subtraction"</li></ul>	What (or whom) creates friction and tension and ignites questioning and doubt? This often adds stress and anxiety with a sense of having to juggle multiple things at the same time. It can feel like things or tasks are constantly being added to your plate, demanding you to do more and be more all at the same time. For example, you must pick up the kids from their after-school activities, make dinner, and not forget to pay the bills. There is unpredictability in the patterns, sometimes with the "division" of people, environments, or situations. Still, they often will leave you exhausted from having to juggle far more than is necessary, even if you can do it successfully. This section is not about ability or capability, it's about how it affects you.

Your objective in this exercise is to conduct an honest self-assessment of your current state. Considering how things may have been in the past may be helpful for additional contexts later on, but it is not the focus of this experiment.

Once you have completed your self-assessment, now comes the time for action. This can be a challenging step. Taking action clears away what isn't serving you (subtracters and dividers) and makes more space for the positive aspects that enhance you and your life (adders and multipliers).

The math assessment provides a clearer picture, bringing awareness and validating information, thoughts, and feelings, and most importantly, guiding prioritized action steps. Sometimes, the "math" is people; other times, it's your internal thoughts or behaviors. It can also include external situations, environments, routines, and habits. You are in the driver's seat of your life, and you can choose to accept the current state or begin taking small actions toward purposeful change.

Overcoming Imposter Syndrome

One of the most common obstacles people will face while finding their perspective is overcoming imposter syndrome. Finding our perspective involves changing our viewpoint, which can sometimes feel like we're becoming a new person. In a way, you are. It's the 2.0 version of you! While this can be exhilarating, it does have moments of uneasiness and doubt.

I have found that when someone feels like they have to overcome imposter syndrome, it often indicates they are at the precipice of making a notable change to discover and embrace their perspective. They have an idea, an action, or an opportunity to forge a new path, and then *whoosh!* There is a wash of dread, doubt, and anxiety. Am I ready for this? Can I do this? Do I have what it takes to succeed? Have I bitten off more than I can chew?

Overcoming imposter syndrome can be the final hurdle when framing your perspective. The final step to lock in that perspective is to say to yourself "Yes, I can! Yes, I will! Watch me!"

The definition of *imposter syndrome* is "a psychological condition that is characterized by persistent doubt concerning one's abilities or accomplishments accompanied by the fear of being exposed as a fraud despite evidence of one's ongoing success" (*Merriam-Webster's Collegiate Dictionary* 2024). This definition highlights the influence and effect on thoughts and emotions as one considers the present and the future.

This is precisely what we do when we clarify and frame our perspective. We gather information from current and past situations, contexts, thoughts, feelings, and doubts. We anticipate where we are headed and consider the target goals we have set for ourselves. Bringing all the pieces together, we clarify and reframe them, framing the possibilities for the future through a new lens.

Overcoming imposter syndrome can best be accomplished by identifying the actions, tasks, and things you can do today that are *low effort* and *high impact.* This would be evidence to support how you *can* reach whatever goal you have set for yourself.

Imposter syndrome is rooted in our emotions and thoughts. When we can demonstrate concretely to ourselves through repeated small actions and behaviors that we *can*, it begins to break down the obstacle. It literally and metaphorically reframes the obstacle into a lesson and an accomplished experience. This builds our self-efficacy, which has a positive ripple effect on the other self-skills. This concept also aligns with the saying "practice makes progress."

I enjoy exercising and different styles of high-impact functional fitness. Usually, six days a week, I start my mornings by exercising. I have found the gym to be a terrific example of watching imposter syndrome sneak in from time to time, even though this is a hobby. Through consistent practice of low-effort, high-impact drills, I reach and, sometimes, pass those target goals. I have done this with gymnastics movements like pull-ups and bar muscle-ups and Olympic weightlifting movements like clean and jerks and snatches. I recall trying to get my very first chin-over-the-bar pull-up. I kept trying to pull my body up, and it would barely budge. I would see other athletes string pull-ups together as strict up-and-down pull-ups or a variation called a "butterfly," where they floated in an effortless circle under the bar. I would try again and get stuck after pulling myself up, less than one inch higher from where I was standing on the ground, under the pull-up bar.

There was no way I could do a pull-up. As a kid, I remember loving to play on the jungle gym at the park and flipping and pulling myself around bars and rings all day. That was over thirty years ago. My time doing pull-ups has, obviously, passed me by. Right? Imposter Syndrome.

The coaches helped me break down the movement into small action drills, building the muscles required to start. I practiced. Then they added onto those drills. I practiced. Fast-forward to now, I am one of those athletes doing the pretty butterfly pull-ups floating in a circle and stringing them together. Imposter syndrome can be overcome with small, intentional action steps. It also helps when you have others to support, encourage, and guide your way as I did in this example with the coaches and my fitness friends.

Turn inward and invest in yourself as a starting point to learn something new, expand your knowledge and skills, and enrich your life. You can overcome imposter syndrome while finding your perspective. You can shift what is in focus and what is genuinely a priority or clarify the importance of any situation's more-significant and minor aspects. This shift can be a powerful catalyst to inspire, define, and launch meaningful change.

> *Mantra: When one door or window closes, (a) it never means they are locked permanently, and (b) it invites opportunities for others to be opened.*

Reflective Questions to Uncover and Frame Your Perspective

It's time to check in with your crossroads experience. Here are some reflective questions you can consider in assisting you to clarify and reframe your perspective:

- Which Essential Elements of Perspective are most influential in your life? How does each help you understand yourself at a deeper level?
- How does this perspective help you move through feeling stuck toward your goals while remaining anchored to your purpose?
- What are the small and intentional habits or actions you are doing daily, weekly, and regularly enough that allow you to recharge or rebalance? Recognize that what worked well for you before this crossroads may no longer serve you in the same way moving forward. That is okay, and it is part of the change process.
- Are you on a negative tidal wave? What speed are you going at right now? Would slowing things down help you to clarify and understand the information around you? Or is it time to speed things up and begin taking small action steps today?
- Is the language, keywords, and phrases you are using balanced and positive? Or have you gained awareness of situations or contexts that may fuel negative language?
- Who are the members of your essential network? How do all of these people pick you up and serve as a source of joy, positivity, support, and love? What or who are negative sources for you in this crossroads experience?
- What is the result of your math assessment? What are the things and who are the people that subtract and deplete

energy from your life? How can you modify and enhance the pieces in your life that enhance the adders and multipliers?
- Are you currently negotiating with yourself while navigating a sense of imposter syndrome?

Use the space below to capture the distilled insights and connect your purpose to your perspective. This act of writing can be the catalyst to clear space, as we reach the final stage of our journey, and fuel your passion. Are you ready to feel the fire?

My Crossroads is _____

My Purpose is _____

The small ways I enhance my life daily include _____

The speed I am at right now is *too fast, need to slow pace just right, keep going too slow, time to move*

My Essential Network Contributors are (list up to the top seven people who are best for you to surround yourself with as you navigate your crossroads):

1. _____
2. _____
3. _____
4. _____
5. _____
6. _____
7. _____

The Negative Language or Negative Tidal Wave occupying space for me right now is often

_____

My Math Function to focus on that is most helpful for me to navigate this crossroads is
_____

As I plan my actionable change,

    my daily tasks are _____
    my short-term goals are _____
    my long-term target goal is _____

STEP III
FUELING PASSION

Fueling passion can be the most exhilarating stage in the process. Yes, you have reached the final step, an accomplishment worth celebrating. Fueling your passion can feel like being in the driver's seat of your favorite car and hitting the gas pedal to the floorboard with the wide-open road in front of you. Let's ride! We can embrace this faster pace with unbridled enthusiasm because we are anchored to a purpose, have a clear perspective, and have goals identified for what we want to achieve and accomplish.

Living your passion elevates your experience to a whole new level within you. It ignites a deeper drive, motivation, and desire you may not have known existed. You are still doing the same hard work, but now everything seems to flow almost effortlessly. It's a comforting and strong feeling of fulfillment. Reassurance and validation that you're doing exactly what you're meant to do. And you are!

We do not see ups and downs as successes and failures when we fuel and live our passion. Instead, we see all experiences, information, and opportunities. When we are up and succeeding, we gather information to reinforce how we act with the intention to meet and reach our current goals. This information can then be used to set, strive, and achieve newer, higher goals, or journey in a new direction of possibilities not yet identified. We see moments others might call plateaus as temporary pauses to check in, reset, take a breath, and then keep climbing with excitement and wonder. We see potential and opportunity for and within others, too. This can amplify our role as an essential network supporter for others. Our positive energy is contagious and can be just the jolt someone else needs, especially if they are at an earlier stage of a crossroads experience.

When we live and fuel our passion, we still experience setbacks or rejections at varying degrees. We can't escape that, and sometimes these setbacks or rejections do suck. Let's be honest about that. This is a normal byproduct of being human.

Here's when we see the unmistakable difference quickly hinting at someone who is living and fueling their passion and someone who is not. The person fueling their passion will interpret that experience as research and information. No matter what occurred, it will not keep them down or even slow their roll. Others might see failure as a reason to give up or significantly pause efforts and actions. A person fueling passion instead sees valuable information to consider, tweaks an action, thought, or emotion, and continues propelling forward with purposeful direction.

For a person fueling passion, they are fine-tuning an instrument or an engine part on a car so it can get to that precise state of optimization. This person says, "Well, that didn't work as planned, but that's okay; let's try again." We continue forward, anchored to our purpose, with a framed perspective that has identifiable target goals, which are specific and measurable and get us excited about what is to come once they are realized!

Writing Your Next Chapter

> *Mantra: "For what it's worth . . . it's never too late or, in my case, to early to be whoever you want to be. There's no time limit." ~F. Scott Fitzgerald*

Fueling your passion requires transformation, which is growth. By reaching this third step, you are evolving into the person you are meant to be—the 2.0 version of you is not just coming, it is here!

It's time to prepare the world for the launch of your newest version. You are like the cell phone, ready to receive updates, strengthening the operating system, enhancing the device with new and efficient features, and improving the overall function of the phone. That is you! Right now! You are plugged in, ready for your software update, and about to receive and install all the new enhancements, features, and tools that will improve functionality and efficiency through an enhanced experience. This is you in your next chapter of life, and the best part is you get to write it!

> *Mantra: "Never give up on what you really want to do. The person with big dreams is more powerful than the one with all the facts." ~Albert Einstein*

One key to writing your next chapter is to start by saying "Yes!" to the experiences and opportunities aligning with your target goal(s). Do not turn down or dismiss an idea. Absorb as much as you can, like a sponge. Take everything in and truly consider the possibilities.

I can hear some of you thinking, *Hang on. If I say yes to everything, won't that knock me out of the balance I worked hard to achieve?* Great question! You won't likely become imbalanced at this stage *because* you completed the hard work earlier. This is why we did the hard work first rather than delay the hard work for later. At this phase, you are anchored to a purpose, driven by a refined and framed perspective, and have a specific target goal, tapped into a well of intrinsic energy and passion, in your sights.

You are not overloading yourself with unnecessary busywork to avoid and distract you from adding meaningful value to your life. Your earlier work has locked your sights on your target goals. This focus innately filters the opportunities, knowing which add value and which are true distractors hindering the needed value. You are working smarter, not harder, with renewed efficiency.

I have a significant amount of personal experience with this as a lifelong learner. I constantly learn new skills, content, and information, fueled by a relentless curiosity. I thrive in environments where I can learn with and from others, and I constantly try to identify, create, or add to these contexts in multiple areas of my life. This is a part of my passion and where I get excited.

When I learn of a new topic, course, or book that will enhance my learning, if it's not related to my current target goals, I put it "on the list." I have a running list of interests to explore. This works as my filter to know when to say yes and when to add something to the list.

As you write your next chapter, optimize your time while maintaining balance. You can be a hard worker and not burn the candle at both ends. You can still achieve your goals. Failure is not bad. Falling or setbacks are not bad. They are learning opportunities.

Stay coachable with a youthful eagerness to grow and learn. Regardless of the success you've had up to that point, be open to absorbing information and perspectives and learning from everyone and anyone. Just because you have accomplishments in the past does not mean you are guaranteed to have an easy path ahead.

During this process, you will build new bridges, repair old ones, and enjoy the views of your favorite ones. These bridges help you navigate between yesterday, today, and tomorrow. As you write your next chapter, it is okay to make a change, building a new bridge to a destination you have not tried before. It is also okay to stay the exact course you were on, making only minor adjustments to navigate that specific crossroads. Not every crossroads will require a massive dose of passion to help navigate through to the other side.

Advanced Math for Everyone

Your time is valuable, and as you tap into your passion, consider how you spend your time and how that passion supports adding value to your time. At this point, you know I like math, so let me offer this advanced math exercise to quantify how valuable your time is. Understanding the value of your time and how it can fuel your personal growth can further motivate you to live your life with purpose, perspective, and passion. Let's break down the numbers.

There are 24 hours in a day, with 60 minutes in each hour. This means you have 1,440 minutes daily to live your life with purpose, perspective, and passion.

Most people spend about one-third of their day sleeping (an average of 8 hours in a 24-hour day). The remaining two-thirds of their day are spent (presumably) awake, alert, and able to engage (an average of 16 hours). We can debate later whether couch surfing and binge-watching your favorite TV show count as "awake and alert." I know for me personally, there are some days when I need that type of day to relax and escape reality.

Back to our math. If you are an active contributor in your life for an average of 16 hours daily, that converts to 960 minutes daily. Here is when it gets exciting—Are you ready?

We have seen how engaging in purpose, perspective, and passion with intentionality can have a positive compounding effect on one's life. It can also have carry-over effects on the members of your essential network.

Would you believe me if I told you that spending as little as 1 percent effort daily during your 16 waking hours will result in significant and compounding levels of impact as you work toward your identified target goals?

This means spending only 9 minutes and 35 seconds daily on a specific task, action, thought, or emotional effort, that aligns with your purpose, perspective, and passion, is the minimum to experience a transformative change in your life. *Less than 10 minutes a day can change your life!*

And wait, there's more! You can intensify the effects when your sleep quality is improved.

How do you make this happen, you ask? I am glad you did! Because this is absolutely within your reach, and you can start today!

Below are suggestions of actionable small steps that you can implement to improve your sleep quality as you write your next chapter. You can implement all of them or pick and choose what works best for the crossroads you are at right now. By engaging in these actions, you will likely identify more actionable strategies that work well for you, and I encourage you to write those down! Different crossroads will require distinct actions to navigate through them.

Suggestions for How to Improve Sleep Quality

Here are the top three ways you can improve your sleep quality, resulting in a positive ripple effect throughout your life:

1. Set a sleep schedule and stick to it.
2. If you can't sleep, get out of bed.
3. Create a calming environment.

1. Set a sleep schedule and stick to it.

To start, consider which days are best to establish a sleep schedule routine. If you are new to a sleep schedule, you may want to begin with weekdays or workdays. Eventually, the goal is to have an established routine that your body can consistently predict every day of the week. Pick a target time of total, uninterrupted sleep between six to eight hours (noting the recommendation for adults is an average of seven hours nightly for maximum sleep quality). Set your parameters for going to bed and waking up. Consider how much time you find most helpful to complete your morning routine. If you know one hour is best to complete your morning routine, then be sure you have reverse engineered your sleep schedule to build in that amount of time (or a little more as a cushion).

For example, if I know I need to leave my house for work by 6:30 a.m. and have one hour for my morning routine, I will set my alarm for 5:00 or 5:15 a.m. This builds in a small cushion of time and ensures I have ample time to get ready each morning before work. Knowing this is the time my alarm will go off, if I want to get seven hours of sleep, I know I need to be closing my eyes around 9:45 to 10:00 p.m. This helps me manage any nightly responsibilities or tasks I need to do, ensuring they're completed or in a permissible state. Many cell phones now have applications built into them that can assist with setting sleep schedules and tracking related biometric data.

2. If you can't sleep, get out of bed.

This habit will help train your body to recognize it's time to sleep when you get into bed. If you head to bed and find you have been lying in bed for twenty to thirty minutes, get out of bed and do something relaxing, ideally in another room. You might listen to calming music or read a book.

Try to avoid anything stimulating or eating food. Whatever you do, do not start doing work. These activities awaken systems in your body. Our objective is to let the biological systems know it is okay to shut down for the night and get some rest. When we retrain our body to understand this routine, we can go to bed and fall asleep soon after our head hits the pillow because our body knows this is the function and goal.

3. Create a calming environment.

Try to keep your bedroom or sleeping areas dark, quiet, and cooler to enhance biological circadian rhythms. This is one reason why watching TV or using a device in bed before sleeping is not recommended. These activities can be stimulating to the mind. Prolonged exposure to light-emitting screens can confuse your body's circadian rhythm as to whether it's daytime or nighttime.

Focusing on quality sleep or improving your sleep by applying one or all three of these suggestions can positively impact your life. It also sets you up to fully live in your passion because you'll have the energy to do so daily.

Suggestions for How to Write Your Next Chapter

Remember, your passions can be diverse and seemingly unrelated. They can provide balance and self-care, enhancing your quality of life. You can make a significant impact without overwhelming yourself by dedicating just 1 percent of your time to each passion, which we mathematically deduced to be less than 10 minutes daily.

I am confident you can commit to spending 9 minutes and 35 seconds daily living your passion. Let's set this up together so you can start today! There is truly no reason to wait another day to get started.

Here are the top four ways you can consider to fuel and live your passion in less than 10 minutes daily:

1. Tell what your most prominent passion is to your essential network.
2. Be adaptable and flexible every day, looking for your signs.
3. Don't hesitate; commit to your passion daily for at least ten minutes.
4. Identify distractors and reprioritize them (or remove them).

Let's break down each of these and see how they can help you realize your goal and evolve into the 2.0 version of yourself you are becoming.

1. Tell what your most prominent passion is to your essential network.

Sharing the news with trusted supporters makes it real and enhances accountability. Each member of your essential network becomes another accountability partner who checks in with you and is interested in learning how you experience your passion.

Remember, the members of your essential network are the individuals you spend the most time around who build you up and celebrate with you, even the smallest wins. They will automatically be interested, invested, and curious about how you realize this passion because they want to see you succeed and live your best life. They already know your value and recognize your true awesomeness. They want the world to know it and will have your back as you showcase your talents. Your essential network helps you remain anchored to your purpose and perspective while blending support, accountability, and an endless supply of untapped energy. They can also recommend other resources, mentors, or influencers that can be helpful to you as you live your passion.

As I began writing this book, I followed a similar path. I had not written a book in this style, which was daunting and scary. I knew it would take a lot of my time and energy, and I was filled with self-doubt (negative inward language). I constantly questioned if I had anything worthwhile to share that people would be interested in hearing (imposter syndrome). I anchored to my purpose of service to help others grow and evolve, and I framed my perspective, reminding myself I am a curious person who loves learning new things and having new experiences. I also knew this goal would be a what-if moment for me if I did not try; life is far too short to give an ounce of energy to wondering *What if?* or having any regrets. So I dove into the proverbial pool's deep end, ready to embrace the challenge and celebrate the undeniable growth and learning I knew would come from this goal, even if I had no clue how it would take shape.

As I started writing, I set my target goals: complete the first draft in one year (long-term target), identify publishers, educate myself about the modalities, research the related types of books already available (short-term goals), and write at least 250 words every other day (daily and immediate tasks).

I leaned on my essential network of people about my new adventure, who leaped with positive support and were ready to be my accountability partners. They would offer constructive feedback along the journey and were excited with me about this new adventure. My passion was in creativity and writing, immersing myself with gusto into a new area of learning rooted in helping and serving others. My intrinsic motivation and genuine excitement were at all-time highs, like the moment Charlie Bucket discovered he had the Golden Ticket, earning a coveted spot to visit the factory and meet Willy Wonka.

After sharing my goals and tasks, purpose, and perspective with my essential network and listening to their instantaneous positive reactions, my self-doubt dissipated even before I started writing. There is a genuine volcano of power among the people in your essential network! Leverage them and bring them in as you traverse your crossroads. You are never alone when you engage with your essential network.

Within days, I had unleashed the fire of passion and was writing daily. Information, ideas, and words poured out of me. I would wake up in the middle of the night, sleepily reaching for my phone or the notepad and pen I keep on the nightstand, squinting my eyes open only as much as was needed to see what I wanted to note before I lost the thought. I was excited to wake up each day and engage in this goal. I never knew where I would finish the day, making each day a mini adventure. I was just as much a part of the creation as the book was itself; we were both evolving simultaneously, and I was the catalyst for it all.

Fueled by my passion and with the support of my essential network, I had fun and was productive while working toward my goals. My network would casually and informally check in to ask, "Hey, how's the book project going?" or "When do you think you'll have a draft of a section ready to read? I'm excited to see what you're putting together and think the idea can help a lot of people." I had support, encouragement, and accountability without judgment and without pressure to define success. Your essential network understands that the process and the experience you are going through are the most rewarding; everything else is the icing on the cake.

My original target of 250 words every other day was overrun by thousands of words daily. My target of one year to complete the rough draft was obliterated, as I finished it in less than one month. I crushed my target goals by engaging my essential network to give me that extra boost, fueling my passion and remaining anchored to my purpose and perspective. I connected with a publishing company within the first week of beginning to write my first draft. Through the process of writing this book, I uncovered the 2.0 version of myself, and I could start to see the positive ripple effect in other areas of my life. The deeper I engaged and committed to myself, the more passion poured from me while writing this book. I became more productive and efficient overall, even with work unrelated to this writing project. I was saying yes a lot. Possibilities, opportunities, and new adventures were what I saw the most. I was saying yes to friends' invitations to grab dinner, check out a farmers' market, or go for a run on a Sunday morning because my language was hyper-positive. *For those who know me, I'm not too fond of running, and it is not my idea of having a fun time. Yet, while* writing this book, I ran with fitness friends weekly, exploring different greenways around our community. I also achieved a new personal record for the farthest distance I have ever run (and probably will ever run for the rest of my life).

> Mantra: "Passion is energy. Feel the power that comes from focusing on what excites you." ~Oprah Winfrey

2. Be adaptable and flexible every day, looking for your signs.

Picture an iceberg. Classically, this image illustrates an exposed small fraction visible to all, while most of the iceberg is hidden under the sea's surface. It can be easy to make assumptions about what we see when we look at the tiny fraction of the iceberg exposed above the surface. If we apply this concept to an individual, people often make assumptions and draw conclusions based on only a tiny fraction of information known or visible about that person: the equivalent of the 10 percent or less of the iceberg overtly visible and exposed above the sea's surface. We typically do not know about the 90 percent or more about that person. We don't know about the time, effort, and energy they spent to get to where they are today. We don't know about their struggles, setbacks, and resilience required for them to reach the point they are at right now. It can be easy, and unintentional, to draw conclusions. Stop and ask yourself, are you forming a conclusion or opinion based on the 10 percent of the iceberg (or information known about a person or situation), or do you have information that taps into the 90 percent below the sea's surface?

This is an unfortunate side effect of the reality TV craze that has distorted our understanding of reality. It produces false narratives of what is a real experience and falsely leads people to believe they are entitled or know all there is to know about another person based only on what they see. It is only the small, edited, and produced information they watch on the TV show.

When you are adaptable and flexible daily, living in your passion and looking for your signs, you are focused on *you*, not others. Your attention is grounded in understanding and adding value to your 90 percent under the sea's surface. You may see and be inspired by other people's 10 percent and absorb that information as ideas. It is not a competition or comparison. Instead, it is a way to be flexible, to consider other approaches and examples while always learning and taking in information and opportunities.

When you are locked into your passion, you will find opportunities to connect with people and experiences within the area you are interested. You will hear about related events that appeared "suddenly." These are breadcrumbs validating you are on the path you are supposed to be on toward your goal. These breadcrumbs of reassurance can add even more fuel to your passion. Stay adaptable and flexible to the signs all around you.

> *Mantra : "We get burned out because we forget* why *we do it, not because of* what *we do." ~Jon Gordon*

3. Don't hesitate; commit to your passion daily for at least ten minutes.

You are ready and called to take action today. There is no point in waiting one minute longer. Remember, the person you are today is not the person you will be in the future. You constantly evolve, and you can't return to who you were before. Embrace this change and keep moving forward.

Starting anything new can be a challenge. Once you have begun, maintaining or building adds layers of challenge, too. Change is a process that can be hard at times. You can do this. I know you can.

I've heard many reasons as to why now is not the right time to start. Why a sense of urgency is not needed; I will admit, I have tried to use some of these reasons, too. Examples are "This week is just too crazy, but next week . . . next week I'll start!" or "I'll start as soon as I have a better sense of my goals; I just haven't decided yet, but I'm excited to make a change" or "I did try, but life got in the way, so now is not the best time, but in another month or three or [pick the timeline], I'll be ready."

I get it—you are busy. You have responsibilities. People depend on you, and time is money. I hear you, and I understand!

I also know the power of the positive ripple effect that will occur when you start fueling and living your passion. Remember the experience I shared when I was writing this book—once I started, I ended up having *more* time and energy available to pour back into every area of my life and engage new ones (like running, *ick*, but it has been such a blast with my fitness friends, yey!). Ultimately, I'm asking you to commit less than ten minutes a day. And if you need help finding those ten minutes, keep reading to identify distractors and reprioritize or remove them altogether.

Mantra : Don't Stop! Don't Quit!

4. Identify distractors and reprioritize them (or remove them).

Just as your perfect strategy will leave those breadcrumbs and clues to guide you toward success, distractors will distort and misdirect you. Distractors will consume your time, attention, focus, and energy. Distractors are not always a dichotomous variable of good and bad either. They are called distractors only for the acknowledgment that they are *distracting* you from reaching your end goals with efficiency. Adulting pummels all of us with distractors by the truckload. We all have them, but not everyone knows how to reprioritize or remove them to optimize their experiences and let that passion shine.

Embrace the idea that you are constantly evolving and improving. You are developing the 2.0 version of yourself. Starting here is a powerful mindset to adopt. This means you must always focus on this important and valuable goal! I have an organizational framework you can apply to inventory and categorize your current state in order to identify distractors, reprioritize those necessary, and remove those that are no longer necessary. Here's what you need to do:

First, start by inventorying any nonnegotiables that must remain constant, no matter your life goals. These might include people such as your family, your partner or spouse, your kids, or people in your essential network who play a crucial role in your personal development. It can also include tasks or actions that help you remain healthy, alert, and ready to engage daily, like exercise, dieting, or sleep habits. Write it down and make that list. Draw a line after the last item to separate these items from the next list we will make.

Second, inventory all you are responsible or accountable for, along with things you enjoy, like hobbies or tasks that take your time and focus. This might include paying bills, grocery shopping, reading at bedtime with the kids, exercising, or cooking and meal prep. Write it down and make this list.

Now, with this second list, go through each item and categorize each as one of the following:

1. Something you can *Retain*
2. Something you can *Automate*
3. Something you can *Delegate*
4. Something you can *Eliminate*

When you choose to Retain an item, you decide to keep it as it is and unchanged. This doesn't mean it is nonnegotiable. It indicates that, at this moment, maintaining the current role or version of this item in your life is the best decision for you. You can always reassess and recategorize it in the future. A common example might be pizza night every Tuesday because you have to work late, and for right now, keeping the routine of picking up pizza on your way home from work every Tuesday is the easiest thing. In the future, that might change and not be a weekly occurrence, or other takeout options might be added to a rotation. But for now, to Retain this routine or habit is best.

Another example I shared is going to the gym for a 5:00 a.m. group class. Right now, this schedule and routine is best for me. There will be a point in the future when attending class at a different time of the day will be optimal. For now, I'm up at 4:10 a.m. bright-eyed and bushy-tailed to get after an intense workout, often before the sun comes up, with my fitness friends.

To Automate is to leverage the growing catalog of technical tools used to streamline your life and buy back your time to refocus on yourself and your goals. A common example is enabling automatic bill payment on recurring monthly bills. Or, setting up a subscription delivery service for everyday household items needed from your favorite store that will ship to your door at a frequency you determine, saving you time to go to the store and sometimes even saving money as some recurring subscription services offer discounts. Another example can be through meal prep services that can save time cooking by delivering completely prepared meals or portioned ingredients with procedure cards to shorten the time to cook a homemade meal. Knowing your current goals and how much beneficial, available time you have can typically be a good starting point for understanding how much to Automate.

To Delegate is to identify tasks and things for others to do who are capable and able of doing them. You may jump in occasionally when needed, but ultimately, others can take the lead. Sometimes, this can be through hiring services like dog walkers, lawn care, or cleaning services. Other times, you can build these into chores for the kids, like unloading the dishwasher or doing laundry.

Finally, to Eliminate is to identify the tasks, responsibilities, or items that no longer serve you. These items are not helpful at this time and, for right now, do not add direct and transparent value to helping you realize your goals. An example might be the need to cancel a subscription to a video streaming service because you are too often sucked into watching shows and find hours are lost each week (or day) in front of the TV. Or, conversely, you are no longer watching TV and spending the money on the subscription service no longer serves you.

Another example might be with email or social media apps on the cell phone. If you feel tethered to your device, removing these apps will help you redirect those precious minutes and hours back into your passion and toward reaching your goals. When you Eliminate, you do so based on the current situation. You may return to the task or item in the future. When you Eliminate, you acknowledge that the return on investment of that item or task does not align with what is best for you as you prepare to unleash the 2.0 version of yourself.

After completing this inventory, categorization, and prioritization exercise, you will find at least ten minutes daily that you can redirect to living in your passion. In fact, you will likely see a lot more than ten available minutes. Reassess your inventory as often as you find helpful. What you need to focus on and how to best optimize your time navigating each crossroads may be different.

Mantra: "Energy flows where attention goes." ~Tony Robbins

Embracing the Change Process

What lights your fire? What excites you? If you could wake up tomorrow and live your best life ever, what would be different from what your life looks like now? Let's make that a reality.

If you were a flower, I want you to bloom where you are planted. You don't need to spend your energy searching for a new flower bed or flowerpot. You are right where you need to be—time to grow and shine! Today there are so many examples of individuals perceived as overnight successes who are now making incredible salaries with what is perceived as little effort. A lot must occur that we often do not see to reach these heights to make it seem effortless.

You can set yourself on a path to being your version of an overnight success, too. How, you ask? Well, I'm glad you did! I do not have the secret sauce for the quick-and-easy path, nor would I put any stock into anyone selling that sauce either. *Easy* now only means *hard* is right around the corner, and most are not prepared for hard when they glide down the easy slide first; the climb up is a lot steeper and more challenging than they're prepared for.

I don't need secret sauce, though, because I know how to navigate the hard first. This is how we uncovered, framed, and fueled our purpose, perspective, and passion. I know how to select the trail to climb and reach new heights, and now, you do too. While others may opt for easy first and slide downward to start their journeys, you and I have gone vertical. When we reach level ground that plateaus, we pause and reset and then continue to climb because we are constantly progressing upward. We are making positive changes, elevating our lives and experiences. Remember, change is constant. How we choose to experience change is up to us.

As you lean into change, it can take any shape and size. Think of it like a microscope and a telescope. Both help you to see the possibilities that can effect change in the future by drawing on different processes and sources of information.

When we examine clarifying information and make actionable strides toward our goal through the lens of a telescope, we look up. We look ahead. We look to the possibilities and wonders that might include educated guesses of the unknown or unproven.

With microscopes, we look down to examine and explore to clarify information. We consider what has already happened as an intentional way to enrich our understanding of the present and to guide future possibilities.

Both telescopes and microscopes have value-added roles in effecting positive transformational change. Either can help identify existing strengths and skills that can transfer to the current crossroads situation you are navigating, supporting your success. Both can illuminate and fuel your passion, propelling you forward with the energy and insights you need.

You have done the hard work, navigated through the ambiguity and possibly darkness, and are actively becoming the 2.0 version of you that you are meant to be. I'm excited for you and all the new possibilities in store for you.

CONCLUSION

Congratulations! You have the knowledge and skills to live your life and navigate crossroads anchored to your purpose, framed by your perspective, and fueled by your passion. These skills and self-applied knowledge will help you navigate any crossroads life may bring.

The older I get, the more I recognize it is rare for a person not to be navigating some form of a crossroads experience. I believe crossroads need not be negative. I hope you can see that too. Even when the context or situation may be less than great, opportunities for learning, growth, enrichment, and love are all still possible.

I've personally experienced the loss of family, loved ones, and friends. I've experienced losing employment and the struggle to find work, wondering if and when bills will be paid. I've experienced a variety of challenging situations where I was bullied, the survivor of gaslighting, and other interpersonal situations. Through all that, I have experienced the unimaginable joy of holding a newborn in my arms while their eyes connect with mine as if to say, "Well, hello! What are we getting up to today?" I've earned promotions, awards, and accolades for innovative contributions to organizations and programs. I've seen and experienced different customs practiced throughout our diverse world. I have loved and been loved and pushed myself to accomplish goals I never could have predicted for myself.

I share this with you, a fellow traveler on the road of life. I know your journey has had twists and turns, too, ups and downs. I know you have navigated challenging crossroads and celebrated extraordinary achievements and fortunes. Whether your crossroads are similar to the ones I've described or they are different, we have both demonstrated courage, resilience, and perseverance to keep going.

You and I do have a lot in common. We believe change is possible. We know that we *can* keep going, even in the darkest days, because deep within us we have a purpose calling for more. We know that while the current situation and crossroads we're navigating is an experience that will influence and inform our decisions, as we look to our respective futures, the experience does not define us. We are the authors of our lives. We are in charge of navigating our journey in life, not other people.

Here is what I know about you (and me):

- You are courageous.
- You are confident.
- You are wise.
- You are a visionary.
- You are creative.
- You have spontaneous wonder.
- You bring a smile to others' faces and have meaningful impacts on the people you connect with.
- You have more to offer the world before your journey ends.
- You know how to recognize that you are at a crossroads and have the skills and strength to navigate it.
- You are a powerful force of positive change with much to offer.

As you continue on your journey, here are key lessons to remember:

1. Anchor to your purpose, which exemplifies your beliefs and values.

   This will help you remain grounded even when you might feel stuck in a quicksand pit in a dark room with no windows. Your purpose is the flashlight in your hand. Pay attention for your Edison Moment to light the way.

2. A helpful way to begin framing your perspective is through examining the situations and contexts from different angles.

   Metaphors can illustrate and remind us to engage specific skills that help us to frame our perspective. They can help us slow down and look at our complete surroundings to understand all of the information available to us from a different viewpoint.

   This action also helps break up the negativity, diminishing its power and space consumed, to make way for positive thoughts and energy. Draw on your unique inner strengths and gifts to clarify your perspective and to point you in the direction that leads you to your next adventure in life. When in doubt, do a little basic math.

3. Failure is a mindset, not a foregone conclusion, and not a definition of yourself.

   You are not a failure, and you do not fail. You have experiences, not failures. You can learn from them, whether their outcomes work the way you planned or not.

Every experience is information you can use to help you successfully navigate this life.

4. You are adaptable and flexible to change, to growth, to evolve.

   You recognize that you will not remain the same tomorrow, and that is okay. Just like a cell phone that goes through upgrades, the core of you remains. Your upgrade includes enhancements, clears away and fixes any bugs, and adds cool new features.

5. You are open to discovering new aspects of yourself because you have the time to do so. All you need is 9 minutes and 35 seconds a day to invest in something new and transform your life.

   Quality sleep will serve you well and maximize your outcomes during those precious minutes. And, once again, do a little more math.

6. You're here to live your best life to its fullest.

   Make every moment count. Try new things and stretch your comfort levels, striving for growth and learning as much as possible. Continue to push yourself to be comfortable with being uncomfortable. Learn from others. Find room and search for people who have reached the goals you aspire to achieve so you can learn directly from them.

   Work smarter, not harder, and you will have time to balance with all the people and things that fill your life with joy, love, and happiness.

Mantra: "I've got this! Yes I can. Yes I will. Watch me." ~Theresa Coogan

Engaging with intentionality to adapt with confidence and flexibility when *Shift Happens* in your life. You don't have to stay stuck or spin your wheels. You can begin making real progress for lasting change with small steps. Turn life's challenges into opportunities for growth by finding your purpose, framing your perspective, and fueling your passion and make change happen today!

THE END

ACKNOWLEDGMENTS

I want to express my gratitude to additional members of my essential network, and the extended essential network, who supported me throughout this journey. Your encouragement kept my spirits high and motivated me to crush my self-imposed goals. I'm grateful for the mini celebrations we shared throughout the process that also fueled me to continue pushing. From pizza or ice cream celebrations at various restaurants around Raleigh when word count deadlines were reached, to trips to the beach without the computer as a reward for reaching key milestones in the process, to telephone and zoom calls celebrating the progress, and so much more, these moments were invaluable. Thanks for sharing in these joyful experiences!

With all my heart, thank you to the following for helping to make this experience come to fruition.

Chandler Bolt and the amazing team at Self-Publishing.com. A special shout out to Kurt Bubna at Self-Publishing.com for his encouragement and guidance through the process and Michael Jarnebro at Vigilant Proofreader for his engaging presence in creating a polished book.

Key members of my essential network who helped keep my energy levels high throughout this process that I'd like to express my deepest gratitude to are:

Christy, one of the first people that encouraged and validated my idea to write this book. I don't know when or if I would have opened a word document and started writing if it wasn't for your encouragement and support. Thank you!

Joe and Mike, the best colleagues and friends a person could ever have. You both have been unwavering supports throughout this entire process cheering me on like I could not have ever imagined. I still recall the afternoon we met for lunch and I shared my idea to write a book. Your reactions of enthusiastic support, followed quickly with comments that validated my idea and wondered aloud why I hadn't already written this book, was a boost of confidence I needed at the vulnerable starting point in the book writing process. Thank you!

Tina and Laura, two of my oldest and dearest friends who are always a phone call away, no matter where I may be. You have both been instrumental sounding boards and supports, as I organized and identified topics and content and navigated the emotional process that is involved with writing a book. Thank you for your encouragement and for sharing the excitement with me from start to finish. I could not have done this without you both.

The many members of my fitness family, cheering me on through this adventure with unbridled enthusiasm in the wee hours of the morning as most people remain blissfully asleep, especially, Mike M., Kyle, Liz, Heidi, Antonio, Benji, Amy, Lucas, Emily, Grant, Griffin, and Mike H.

And last, but certainly not least, the endless love and support from my dog, Maze, shared through snuggle time on the couch while I worked on the laptop, or walks on the greenway that sometimes involved me talking out loud to her or myself as I fleshed out ideas. Maze was also instrumental in forcing me to take breaks from the computer to run around and play, which we know is essential to the process. Thank you, sweet girl!

AUTHOR BIO

Dr. Theresa Coogan is a licensed counselor, coach, educator, speaker, and consultant with a wealth of experience across various industries and sectors. A lifelong learner, she is committed to expanding her knowledge through reading, training, and skill development, enabling her to effectively serve diverse audiences.

Dr. Coogan's expertise spans a wide range of topics, including health and wellness, personal development, educational strategies, business and entrepreneurship, risk management, and mental health counseling. With her Lean Six Sigma Black Belt, she specializes in efficiency strategies that drive meaningful change in organizations and individuals alike.

Outside of her professional endeavors, she enjoys quality time with her family and her spirited rescue Pitbull, Maze, spending as much time as possible in the sunshine and exploring the outdoors of Raleigh, North Carolina. She is a regular member of the 5AM crew at the gym most mornings, and enjoys winding down each day reading.

While she has previously published articles, papers, book chapters, and academic texts, this nonfiction book marks an exciting new chapter in her writing journey. Dr. Coogan looks forward to exploring themes of interpersonal and intrapersonal development, practical strategies for meaningful change, and their implications for health, career, and relationships in her future books.

OTHER BOOKS BY THERESA COOGAN, PH.D.

This book is the first nonfiction publication by Theresa. With a strong foundation in academic and research journal articles published in peer-reviewed journals, she has also delivered numerous presentations, trainings, and workshops, and authored both academic books and chapters in edited books.

To learn more, visit the Resources & More page at:
www.tacticalchanges.com

URGENT PLEA!

Thank You for Reading My Book!

I appreciate feedback and
I am interested to hear what you have to say.

I need your input to make the next version of
this book and my future books better.

Please take two minutes now to leave a helpful review on

Amazon letting me know what you thought of the book.

Thanks so much!
Theresa

Made in United States
North Haven, CT
19 January 2025

64649777R10083